H²h
ow to Help

ADHD and Attention Difficulties
How to Help

Fintan O'Regan
and Sara Cave

ADHD and Attention Difficulties

© Pavilion Publishing & Media

The authors have asserted their rights in accordance with the Copyright, Designs and Patents Act (1988) to be identified as the authors of this work.

Published by:
Pavilion Publishing and Media Ltd
Blue Sky Offices, 25 Cecil Pashley Way
Shoreham by Sea, West Sussex
BN43 5FF

Tel: 01273 434 943
Email: info@pavpub.com
Web: www.pavpub.com

Published 2022

A catalogue record for this book is available from the British Library.

ISBN: 978-1-91341412-2

Pavilion Publishing and Media is a leading publisher of books, training materials and digital content in mental health, social care and allied fields. Pavilion and its imprints offer must-have knowledge and innovative learning solutions underpinned by sound research and professional values.

Authors: Fintan O'Regan and Sara Cave
Cover design: Emma Dawe, Pavilion Publishing and Media Ltd
Page layout and typesetting: Tony Pitt, Pavilion Publishing and Media Ltd
Printing: CMP

Contents

Series Preface

Young people in today's society face considerable stresses. The Prince's Trust, which has monitored youth opinion for ten years, found that just under half of young people who use social media now feel more anxious about their future when they compare themselves to others on websites and apps such as Instagram, Twitter and Facebook. A similar proportion agreed that social media makes them feel 'inadequate'. The *Guardian Weekly* noted in early 2019 that more than half of young people think that social media creates 'overwhelming pressure' to succeed.

There are many issues that are likely to affect every pupil at some point during his or her time at school. How these are dealt with can be 'make or break' for some pupils, because of the crucial stages in education that can be affected. The implications are deep and broad because, understandably, the child's experience of education, and his or her success at school, can have a tremendous impact on later life chances.

The *How to Help* series covers a broad and comprehensive range of topics that will have resonance for today's parents, carers and educators. Each title is designed to make a valuable contribution in the breadth of issues that it introduces, and the realistic helping strategies that it puts forward.

Gavin Reid and Jennie Guise
Series Editors

About the Authors

Fintan O'Regan is a Behaviour and Learning Consultant and Trainer who works nationally and internationally with schools and school support systems to design management strategies for children and families struggling with Special Educational Needs and Disabilities (SEND) and behaviour issues. From 1996-2002 he was Head Teacher of the Centre Academy, the UK's first school for students aged 7-19 to specialise in issues related to Attention Deficit Hyperactivity Disorder (ADHD), Autism Spectrum Disorder (ASD) and Oppositional Defiant Disorder (ODD). Fin has written a number of books and articles on these subjects and across a range of learning, behaviour and socialisation issues.

Sara Cave is Specialist Teacher for the Specialist Teaching and Learning service in Ashford, Kent, advising and supporting mainstream schools and working in partnership with schools, parents and agencies to build capacity for inclusive practice for neurodivergent students who may face barriers in accessing the curriculum in their settings. Prior to this role, Sara was a Special Educational Needs Coordinator (SENCO) in a village primary school. She has a wide range of classroom experience working with and supporting children with attention difficulties, as well as experience of leading support and provision for children in an advisory and leadership capacity as SENCO and Senior Leadership Team (SLT) member.

Authors' Preface

The two authors of this book first met at an ADHD training course that took place at specialist school in Kent. Fin ran the course, and Sara attended as a delegate and contributed to a number of discussions regarding teaching students with ADHD throughout the day. Chatting afterwards, we found that we had much in common in terms of supporting children with ADHD. Some years later, when the opportunity arose to write this book, we thought it was the perfect opportunity to share our skills, knowledge and experience.

The key issue that we agreed on that day, and that we still agree on now, is that there is no such thing as a typical 'ADHD child' – there are only children with ADHD. Attention Deficit Hyperactivity Disorder is a complex and somewhat controversial condition; however, the fact is that its symptoms or traits are very real, and they affect children, adolescents and adults around the globe in a range of different ways. With that in mind, the central aim of this book is to help teachers and parents demystify ADHD and gain an insight into understanding how individuals with attention difficulties may view the world. We also explain that many individuals with ADHD have a range of overlapping conditions and traits, which means that supporting them is often not straightforward.

We have both dug deep into our years of experience and expertise to cover a wide range of practical approaches to help children and families in terms in learning, behaviour and socialisation issues. In Part 5, we also draw directly on the experience of seven mothers, for whose participation and willingness to share their stories we are extremely grateful. We hope over the course of this book to provide you with some proven ideas and strategies, confirm some existing practices, and best of all spark some innovative new approaches for supporting children and young people with impulsivity, inattention and hyperactivity issues – otherwise known as ADHD.

We look forward to you joining us on the journey.

Fin O'Regan
Sara Cave

How to Use This Book

Topics in this *How to Help* book are organised within five major sections, comprising Parts 2 to 5:

- Learning and school
- Supporting behaviour for learning
- Working in partnership with others
- ADHD at home

Within these sections, each topic is discussed in a separate chapter (although it should be noted that in practice there will frequently be areas of overlap), with advice for parents, carers, teachers and schools. You can read through the sections in order or go straight to what concerns you most. The topics have been chosen to represent the key issues that typically arise when seeking to understand, parent, teach and support children and young people with ADHD.

 Whenever you see the *How to Help* icon, you can expect to find practical, ready to use suggestions and strategies for helping children and young people to mitigate and manage the issues and symptoms associated with ADHD and attention difficulties.

We recommend that you read in full the Introduction (Part 1) and the Conclusion (Part 6). The former serves as an entry point into the main chapters, presenting the subject and core principles relating to it along with a list of ten essential things to know. The latter summarises the most important points for readers to take away, and offers final comments for parents, carers, teachers and schools.

To keep up to date with the *How to Help* series, bookmark:

www.pavpub.com/howtohelp

"Learn from yesterday, live for today, hope for tomorrow. The important thing is not to stop questioning."

Albert Einstein

Part 1: Introduction

Chapter 1: What is ADHD?

Introducing ADHD and attention difficulties

Attention is a word that means notice taken of someone or something interesting or important. Some people are naturally better at paying attention than others, and some individuals seem to find certain things much less interesting than other people. With this in mind, the key questions that should concern us as parents, carers, teachers and schools are: 1. Why do some people have better attention skills than others?; 2. Why are some things less interesting to some people than to others?; and 3. How can we help those who struggle to pay attention?

In this book we will consider some of the general reasons for attention difficulties, and some of the broad challenges that arise from them. Part 4 will look in depth at the challenges of attention difficulties within the home. Most of all, though, we will focus on how to support individuals who struggle with attention issues when trying to learn in a school setting.

The term generally given to describe attention difficulties in children and adults is Attention Deficit Hyperactivity Disorder (ADHD). ADHD is an internationally validated condition of brain dysfunction, in which individuals have difficulties in controlling impulses, inhibiting appropriate behaviour and sustaining attention. The net result is usually educational, behavioural, social and related difficulties.

The full diagnostic criteria regarding ADHD are listed in specialist manuals designed for used by qualified professionals (see Chapter 3 and Appendix 1) and are not intended to be accessible or helpful to the general public. However, the 'triad' of core features of ADHD may be described as follows:

1. Poor attention span
2. Excessive impulsivity
3. Hyperactivity

Symptoms of a poor attention span may include being disorganised, being forgetful, being easily distracted and finding it difficult to sustain attention in tasks or play activities. Symptoms of impulsive behaviour or hyperactivity may include fidgeting, interrupting others, having trouble playing quietly and always being on the go. While we all exhibit such behaviours from time to time, and many children and young people go through phases where they can be inattentive or restless, the key difference in ADHD is the degree and intensity to which they occur in specific individuals.

Further confusing the situation is the fact that other Specific Learning Difficulties (SpLDs) such as dyslexia (difficulties with reading), dyspraxia (difficulties with physical coordination, more accurately known today as Developmental Coordination Disorder), dysgraphia (difficulties with writing) and dyscalculia (difficulties with numbers and arithmetic) also occur in approximately 40% of children with ADHD.

While the academic and behavioural issues associated with ADHD are high on school agendas, an important area of concern regarding children with attention issues is their interaction with others. Initially, pupils with traits of ADHD can appear quite amusing within a group of learners, but this 'class clown' effect soon wears thin to be replaced by impatience and intolerance of the constant interruptions that can take place. This can lead to isolation of the individual from the group.

In addition, many problems for children with traits of ADHD stem from their inability to handle the various kinds and levels of distractions that they may encounter in their immediate surroundings. This is why children with ADHD tend to do best in a consistent and structured environment that provides them with the safety and security they need to stay focused and on task.

The symptoms of ADHD usually improve with age but can continue into adult life. Sometimes ADHD is not recognised or diagnosed until the person is an adult. Often the symptoms change, with less over-activity but more risk-taking, lack of concentration and impulsivity. This can make it hard for some adults with ADHD to get along with other people, learn effectively, and perform well at work.

A brief history of attention difficulties

While the condition we know today as 'ADHD' is a relatively new concept, the underlying issues and behaviours are certainly not new.

Excessively hyperactive, inattentive, and impulsive children were described as long ago as the late eighteenth century, when the Scottish physician Sir Alexander Crichton described a 'morbid alteration of attention' as "The incapacity of attending with a necessary degree of constancy to any one subject."[1] Fifty years later, the German physician Heinrich Hoffman wrote children's a story about 'Fidgety Phil', a "naughty, restless child" who is asked to "sit still for once at table" but instead fidgets so much that his chair falls over, he pulls the cloth from the table and the family dinner is ruined.[2]

The starting point of ADHD as we know it today is generally seen as being in lectures given in 1902 by the English paediatrician Sir George Still. He described "an abnormal defect of moral control in children" and found that some affected children, while intelligent, could not control their behaviour in the way a typical child would.[3] Then in 1937, the German physicians Franz Kramer and Hans Pollnow described "a hyperkinetic disease of infancy". They noted an urgent character to the motor activity of affected children, who could not stay still, liked to run and climb and were unhappy when prevented from doing so.[4]

Expert View

"I would point out that a notable feature in many of these cases is a quite abnormal incapacity for sustained attention."

Sir George Still.

Around the same time as Kramer and Pollnow's work, the American psychiatrist Charles Bradley administered benzedrine sulphate, an amphetamine that had recently been approved for medical use in the USA, to ease headaches in a children's home in Rhode Island. He discovered that, unexpectedly, his young patients' behaviour and performance in school improved as a side-effect of the medicine; however his findings were largely ignored, and it was not until many years later than doctors and researchers belatedly recognised the importance of his discovery. Eventually, this work led to the development of medications such as Ritalin, widely used to manage ADHD today.

1   Crichton, A. (1798) An inquiry into the nature and origin of mental derangement: comprehending a concise system of the physiology and pathology of the human mind and a history of the passions and their effects.

2   Hoffmann, H. (1846) Der Struwwelpeter. Oder lustige Geschichten und drollige Bilder für Kinder von 3 bis 6 Jahren. Loewes, Stuttgart: Frankfurter Originalausgabe.

3   Still, G.F. (1902). Some abnormal psychical conditions in children: the Goulstonian lectures. Lancet. 1: 1008-1012.

4   Kramer F. & Pollnow, H. (1932) Über eine hyperkinetische Erkrankung im Kindesalter. Aus der Psychiatrischen und Nerven-Klinik der Charité in Berlin. Mschr Psychiat Neurol. 82:21-40.

The American Psychiatric Association issued its first *Diagnostic and Statistical Manual of Mental Disorders* (commonly known to professionals as 'the DSM') in 1952, listing all the recognised mental health disorders along with their causes, risk factors and treatments. ADHD was not listed, but in 1968 the second edition of the DSM included 'Hyperkinetic Impulse Disorder' for the first time. The third edition of 1980 changed the name to 'Attention Deficit Disorder' (ADD) and finally this was revised in 1987 to 'Attention Deficit Hyperactivity Disorder'. However the condition was still poorly understood and under-researched, and it was not until the DSM's fourth edition of 1994 that the description of ADHD began to resemble more closely the condition we recognise today.

Within the UK, ADHD only began to gain acceptance as a recognised condition in 2000 when the first National Institute of Health and Care Excellence (NICE) report on the condition was published. Before this, there were widespread doubts as to its very existence, and the focus was on hyperactivity and impulsiveness rather than attention as a key issue for children. In 1990, only forty children in the whole of the UK were being treated for ADHD; today there are tens of thousands. There was virtually no recognition of the far-reaching impact of the condition on education and mental health, or that it could persist into adulthood.

A word on medication

Medication is often one of the first treatments suggested to manage ADHD, although psychological treatments such as cognitive behavioural therapy (CBT) have an increasing role. However, many families react with doubt or fear to the suggestion that their child should take medication, and it will always be a controversial area. Medication cannot cure ADHD, and some children will experience side-effects, but with careful monitoring and management the use of medication can have positive effects in reducing symptoms and enabling children to concentrate and learn more effectively.

Treatments for ADHD comprise stimulants and non-stimulants. Stimulants include methylphenidate (sold under brand names including Ritalin) and lisdexamfetamine (sold under brand names including Vyvanse). Non-stimulants include atomoxetine and guanfacine. We will look at the pros and cons of medication in more detail in Part 4 of this book. For now, it is enough to say that medication is one possible and potentially beneficial component in a much wider package of support for a child with ADHD.

Chapter 2: Causes and consequences

What causes ADHD and how common is it?

Just as there is no single best strategy for managing ADHD, so there is no single identifiable cause. Like many developmental issues, ADHD appears to have multiple causal components. Evidence from research suggests that neurological, genetic and environmental factors all contribute to the condition.

Neurological factors:	A number of research studies by world-renowned expert Russell Barkley have suggested that parts of the brain (frontal and parietal lobes and part of the mid-brain) do not perform as well as they should in children with ADHD.[5] In particular, communication between the frontal lobes (which are responsible for executive function) and the parietal lobes (where action is initiated) may be slower to mature than in children who are not affected by attention difficulties.
Genetic factors:	ADHD is among the most genetically influenced (i.e. inherited) of psychological disorders. If there is a child with ADHD in a family, then there is a 45% chance that at least one parent has the disorder and a 30% chance that another sibling may also be affected. For identical twins, the chance increases to around 85%. Scientists are now searching for the genes that contribute to this disorder.
Environmental factors:	Though neurological and genetic factors appear to be at the root of ADHD, environmental factors (i.e. those factors arising from the young person's surroundings) cannot be ignored as they are critical to development. The evidence suggests that ADHD is unlikely to develop purely from social factors like poor parenting, family stress, divorce, excessive screen time or poor diet, although some or all of these factors may potentially lead to wider difficulties and/or contribute to problematic behaviours.
Developmental injury:	In a small percentage of cases, ADHD seems to arise as a result of developmental injury to the relevant brain regions. This might be due to maternal use of alcohol or tobacco during pregnancy, premature delivery with associated minor brain haemorrhage, or accidental head injury after birth.

---

5   Barkley, R.A. (1997). Attention-deficit/hyperactivity disorder, self-regulation, and time: toward a more comprehensive theory. *Journal of Developmental and Behavioral Pediatrics* 18:271–279.

ADHD occurs in approximately 3-9% of school aged children. Cases began to escalate significantly in the 1990s. This may have been driven by rising awareness among parents of ADHD, leading to more reporting of symptoms, along with an increase in efficiency of referral and diagnosis among teachers and doctors. These factors make it unclear whether the incidence of ADHD itself was or is actually increasing.

Most research studies confirm a male-to-female ratio of 3:1 for ADHD. However, research on gender differences suggests that girls may be consistently underdiagnosed, partly because of differences in how their ADHD is expressed. Girls with ADHD are reported to have fewer hyperactive/impulsive symptoms and more inattentive symptoms compared to boys.[6] Furthermore, girls with ADHD present more commonly with the inattentive subtype. Because their behaviour is less disruptive, girls may not be referred for ADHD assessment as often as boys. This may lead to underdiagnosis and a lack of appropriate treatment for girls struggling with attention issues.

Another contributing factor to late or missed diagnoses in girls is the presence of co-existing issues that can cloud the diagnostic picture. As many as 75% of children with ADHD are likely to have at least one other diagnosable condition. Boys with ADHD generally have more externalizing (outwardly directed) disorders than other boys, while girls with ADHD may show more internalizing (inwardly directed) disorders. Often other diagnoses are made long before ADHD is assessed in girls; by contrast, more overt acting out behaviour seems to drive referral for ADHD assessment in boys.

What does ADHD look like and how long does it last?

It is well documented that ADHD is a chronic, debilitating disorder which may impact upon many aspects of a person's life including education, social skills and parent-child relationships. Children with the disorder are proven to be at greater risk for longer term negative outcomes such as lower educational and employment attainment. All of this will be in the mind of any parent whose child has been newly diagnosed. The most pressing question for those new to ADHD, however, is likely to be how the disorder affects everyday life. Children typically spend less than 25% of their time away from their families, so the true impact of ADHD is often felt more forcefully at home than at school.

6   Gershon, J. (2002) A meta-analytic review of gender differences in ADHD. *Journal of Attention Disorders* 5(3):143-154.

Children and young people with ADHD are characterised by a phenomenon known as 'consistent inconsistency.' On some days they can produce great work unassisted and within the allotted time; on others, they struggle to stay on task and even with close supervision may not accomplish much. Their erratic performance perplexes teachers and parents and can create the impression of laziness.

Expert View

"The problem is not that they cannot do the work, but that they cannot maintain this persistent productivity the way others can."

Russell A. Barkley

It is not perfectly understood why those with ADHD show this striking pattern of inconsistency in their behaviour and productivity. However, it is likely to be due to the core impairment of impulse control. Consistent levels of productivity require the ability to inhibit impulses to engage in other activities. Therefore, the more limited or erratic a pupil's impulse control is, the more variable their performance will be.[7] It follows from this that 'executive functioning' of the brain, which involves planning, controlling and regulating one's activity, is impaired as a result of the core issues associated with ADHD, and that as a result of this individuals may have significant difficulties with self-management or self-regulation.

It is important to remember that children, adolescents and even adults with ADHD are not always inattentive or easily distracted; they are also capable of focusing very intently on things that hold a particular interest for them. In fact they can get so absorbed that they are oblivious to the world around them and the passage of time, spending hours playing a computer game or surfing the Internet. This hyper focus, like distractibility, is thought to be related to a dopamine deficiency in the brain's frontal lobes. Dopamine is a hormone that is important in a range of ways throughout the brain and body, and the frontal lobes of the brain control important cognitive skills including the regulation of attention. While they are at opposite ends of the spectrum, distractibility and hyper focus both represent problems in the regulation of the attention system in ADHD.[8]

Children with ADHD can also find it hard to 'shift gears'. They will tend to persist in behaviours or activities they enjoy long after others would have moved on, and they appear to be drawn to things that give instant feedback. If it can be harnessed, the ability to hyper focus can be an asset. Some youngsters with ADHD are able to channel this onto something productive, such as a school project. For others, the chance to focus on

---

7   Barkley, R. A. (1997) *ADHD and The Nature of Self-Control*. New York: Guilford Press.

8   Barkley, R. A. (2006). *Attention-deficit hyperactivity disorder: A handbook for diagnosis and treatment* (3rd ed.). New York: Guilford Press.

a preferred topic or activity can be used as a reward or motivator for completing a less interesting but important task.[9]

The disorder develops in childhood, usually by the age of five or even sooner, and is highly persistent across development in most, though not all, cases. Studies suggest that 80% of children diagnosed with ADHD in childhood continue to be impaired by the disorder in adolescence, and that up to 67% continue to have symptoms producing impairment as adults.

Dealing with a diagnosis

An ADHD diagnosis is not a sentence for a lifetime of suffering. It is true that some individuals do have serious and pervasive problems, but others experience only mild symptoms. The good news is that ADHD is a treatable condition and early intervention can lead to successful outcomes. It is normal for parents and carers to feel a degree of upset or intimidation when their child is diagnosed with ADHD; however, getting a diagnosis can also be the first step toward making life better. As with many things, once you know what you are up against you can start to deal with it – which means taking control of symptoms and feeling more confident in every area of life.

Regardless of where your child is on this spectrum, there are many steps you can take to manage the symptoms. One important practical step for parents is to join a support group where you can meet others who are going through a similar journey and share information, strategies and success stories. Another is to work as closely as possible with your child's school, and sometimes other relevant agencies, in order to fully meet your child's behaviour, socialisation and learning needs.

An ADHD diagnosis may feel like a label, but it may be more helpful to think of it as an explanation. It explains why children have struggled with life skills such as paying attention, following directions, listening closely, and being organized – things that come easily to other people. So a diagnosis can be a relief: parents can rest easier knowing that it wasn't laziness or a lack of intelligence standing in their child's way, but a disorder that you can work together to learn how to manage.

---

9   Kohlberg, J. & Nadeau, K. (2002) *ADD-Friendly Ways to Organize Your Life.* New York: Brunner-Routledge.

Chapter 3: Assessment and diagnosis

How is ADHD diagnosed?

As we have said, the typical hallmarks of children who are diagnosed with ADHD are a lack of focus, poor self-control, impulsivity, inappropriate behaviours and being easily distracted. However, these symptoms are not necessarily seen to the same degree in all children diagnosed. As a result, clinicians currently recognise three sub-types of the disorder:

1. The predominantly hyperactive-impulsive type
2. The predominantly inattentive type
3. The combined type, which describes the majority of cases

In order to diagnose ADHD the clinician must make an assessment, in the course of which he or she must be able to note the presence of six or more of the nine symptoms listed below for either inattention or hyperactivity/impulsivity. In addition, these symptoms must have persisted for at least six months and be inconsistent with the child's developmental level, some significant degree of impairment must be present in two or more settings (e.g. home and school), and some of the symptoms must have been present before the age of seven. The symptoms also should not be due to another disorder, and there must be evidence of a significant level of impairment in social, academic or occupational functioning.

Figure 1.1.: The specific symptoms of different types of ADHD (adapted from the DSM-5)[10]

Inattention:	■ Pays little attention to detail in schoolwork or other activities; makes careless mistakes. ■ Frequently has problems in sustaining attention (e.g. staying focused in lessons or reading a lengthy text). ■ Often seems not to be listening when spoken to directly. ■ Often does not follow instructions and fails to finish tasks. Has difficulty organising tasks and achieving good time management. ■ Avoids and dislikes tasks which demand sustained mental effort. ■ Constantly loses things. ■ Is easily distracted. ■ Often forgetful.
Hyperactivity:	■ Squirms and fidgets in seat; often restless. ■ Often out of seat when staying seated is required. ■ Often runs around or climbs excessively in situations where this is inappropriate. Has difficulty playing quietly. ■ Constantly 'on the go'. ■ Talks excessively.
Impulsivity:	■ Blurts out answers before the questions have been completed. Often has difficulty with turn-taking. ■ Frequently interrupts or intrudes on others' conversations or games.
The three major types of ADHD:	■ Hyperactive-impulsive (where six or more hyperactive-impulsive, but five or fewer inattentive symptoms have been present for the past six months) ■ Inattentive (six or more inattentive, but three-five hyperactive-impulsive symptoms have been present for the past 6 months Restrictive inattention (six or more inattentive, but two or fewer hyperactive-impulsive symptoms have been present for the past 6 months ■ Combined (6 or more hyperactive –impulsive symptoms have been present for the past 6 months)

10   American Psychiatric Association. (2013). *Diagnostic and Statistical Manual of Mental Disorders (5th ed.)*. Arlington, VA: APA.

The challenges of assessment

ADHD frequently occurs in combination with other issues, which makes its identification a complex process. The assessor needs to build a picture of the pupil across a number of contexts and over extended timelines, and as a result there is no one conclusive test for ADHD. No single professional can reach a valid diagnosis without the gathering of information from a range of sources and consideration of the contributions of key people in the child's life.

Central to the process are the accounts of parents, teachers and, where appropriate, the individual concerned. The purpose is not only to arrive at a diagnosis but also, crucially, to identify the child's strengths, skills and talents as these will form the basis of successful interventions both in school and in other contexts. The emphasis should never be exclusively on problems.

The process of assessment for ADHD typically includes some or all of the following elements:

- Direct observation
- Clinical interviews
- Behavioural checklists
- Educational reports
- Involvement of parents
- Medical testing

Direct Observation

Real life samples of a child's behaviour are invaluable, and we know that many parents and teachers feel that seeing a child in the clinic only tells half the story. Psychologists and other professionals will gain most by observing the child in as natural a setting as possible, and ideally across a range of different settings to include home, school, outside play and so on.

Clinical interviews

A series of in-depth interviews should be undertaken with the child's parents or carers, yielding a detailed history of his or her birth, development, personality, relationships, functioning across a range of settings and current problems. A less-structured interview is then held with the young person. This might involve different play activities and sometimes more structured tasks to assess concentration, attention, impulsivity and problem-solving, and cognitive style. Other significant people in the child's life may also be interviewed, including siblings, grandparents and childminders.

These interviews are regarded as the single most important part of any assessment, because it is through them that a clinician can discern if pervasive patterns of inattention, impulsivity and/or hyperactivity are present or if the problems causing concern are due to other factors. The aim is to combine multiple perspectives to gain as clear a picture of the individual young person as possible.

Behavioural Checklists

Several behavioural checklists or rating scales are routinely used to obtain reliable, valid and comparable accounts of a child or adolescent's behaviour. These standardised questionnaires are completed by key people, usually parents and teachers, and by the student himself/herself.

Among the most commonly used checklists are the **Conners Parent and Teacher Rating Scales**[11] which are available in both long and short forms. Factors identified by the teacher's version include hyperactivity, conduct problems, emotional overindulgence, asocial behaviour, daydreaming and attentiveness. The Conners scale helps to differentiate ADHD into the three main forms – Impulsive Hyperactive, Inattentive or Combined. The Conners Abbreviated Symptom Questionnaire is a supplementary ten item checklist that is typically used to measure the response to treatment interventions.

Based on the same clinical expertise, research skills and theoretical knowledge used to develop the scale for children and adolescents, the **Conners' Adult ADHD Rating Scales** (CAARS) are designed to help assess, diagnose and monitor the treatment of ADHD in adults. Two formats are included; for self-report ratings and observer ratings. Both the self-report and observer forms provide multimodal assessments of the same behaviours and problems, and contain an identical set of scales, subscales and indexes. CAARS forms are available in long, short and screening versions. A new user's guide enables the instrument to also be used effectively with correctional (prison) populations.

Other instruments include the Achenbach **Child Behaviour Checklist**[12], and the **Home Situations and School Situations Questionnaires**.[13] The Achenbach is a wide-ranging assessment looking at a range of behaviours. It is considered the first step in the screening process for ADHD, and

---

11   Connors, C. K. (1997). *Conners' Rating Scales-Revised Technical Manual*. North Tonawanda, NY.

12   Achenbach, T. M. (1991). Manual for the Child Behavior Checklist/4-18 and 1991 profile. Burlington, VT: University of Vermont, Department of Psychiatry.

13   Barkley, R. A. (1981). *Hyperactive children: A handbook for diagnosis and treatment*. New York: Guilford Press.

is generally followed up with a more ADHD-specific assessment tool. Another recommended rating scale is the **Attention Deficit Disorder Evaluation Scale** (ADDES-5).[14] It can be used to screen children aged 2-18 and its main advantage is that it is directly linked to interventions presented in a 'cookbook' type format (i.e. the assessment result leads directly to a recommended intervention).

Behaviour rating scales serve a critical function in the identification and diagnosis of ADHD, but they should only be used as part of a broader, multimodal assessment.[15] This is because understanding the context within which behaviour occurs is critical to an accurate diagnosis.

Educational reports

Information from the child's school is critical not only to the diagnosis itself, but also in terms of assessing the impact of the disorder on the child's educational experience and progress. As well as the current situation, past school performance and behaviour are also relevant. The type of information that teachers can provide includes assessment and examples of the child's:

- Attention span
- Listening skills
- Social behaviour
- Work rate/completion,
- On-task behaviour
- Reaction to correction and instruction
- Level of organisation and planning
- Memory
- Level of aggression
- Personality
- Learning difficulties
- Strengths

Both formal and informal reports should be sought, and ideally the child's teacher or head of year should be consulted by the diagnosing professional. When providing this information, education professionals should take great care to remain objective and avoid exaggerating

---

14   McCarney, S.B. & House, S.N. (2019). *Attention Deficit Disorder Evaluation Scale* (ADDES-5). Columbia, MO, Hawthorne Educational Services.

15   Power, T. J., & Ikeda, M. J. (1996). The clinical utility of behavior rating scales: Comments on the diagnostic assessment of ADHD. *Journal of School Psychology*, 34(4), 379-385.

experiences in an effort to support a possible diagnosis. Students should always be compared to their average peers, with the task, the context and the demands of the specific classroom in mind.

Parental involvement

The role of the parent or carer is absolutely crucial in the testing process. The parent or carer knows the child best, is the child's greatest advocate and their most important source of support. If you are a parent or carer in an assessment process, your roles are both emotional and practical. You can:

- Provide emotional support for your child throughout the diagnostic process
- Ensure that your child sees the right specialist and obtain a second opinion if necessary
- Provide unique and helpful information for doctors/specialists, including open and honest answers to questions about your child's history and current situation
- Monitor the speed and accuracy of the evaluation process

It is important to be mindful that the tools used for diagnosis, as well as the overall length of the assessment process, will differ from specialist to specialist. Parents should therefore be mindful of this, and be prepared for the fact that the outcome may not be as expected.

Medical Testing

In the case of young children, a referral for paediatric medical investigation should also form part of the assessment. The purpose of this is to rule out the presence of any co-existing disorder which may complicate or account for the child's symptoms. For example, children are routinely checked for visual or hearing problems. Where a child has other difficulties in addition to ADHD, these must be identified and treated in parallel. A medical screening is also essential for older students and adults, especially where medication is considered as a component of any intervention.

Chapter 4: Overlapping issues

Overlap is the norm, not the exception

Many children with ADHD have other problems with learning. In fact, when learning disorders are defined as resulting in "performance significantly below the expected level", 75% of children with ADHD meet this criterion while still in primary education.[16] However, when narrower definitions are used, such as academic achievement relative to intellectual functioning, the number can drop to 2.5% or less.[13] Problems of cognitive or intellectual functioning may be a common factor underpinning both the ADHD and the learning difficulties, while the ADHD and its associated conduct problems may in turn lead to poor academic performance.

Almost any emotional or behavioural condition can potentially overlap with ADHD (or be comorbid with ADHD, to use the scientific term). In the section below, we will offer short descriptions of some of the most commonly encountered ones, with particular reference to the extent and impact of their co-occurrence with ADHD.

Commonly co-occurring conditions

Autism Spectrum Disorder (ASD)

Autism is characterized by difficulty in communicating and forming relationships, and in using language and abstract concepts. Some early symptoms are extreme sensory sensitivities, lack of social skills or a preference to be alone, poor understanding of abstract language, and obsessive interests. Early detection and treatment of autism is important, but because the symptoms of ASD and ADHD can overlap, diagnosing and separating the two disorders can be difficult.

The most recent edition of the *Diagnostic and Statistical Manual of Mental Disorders* (or DSM, which we introduced in Chapter 1) opened the possibility of diagnosing an individual with both ADHD and ASD. This was not the case before. Studies show that up to 50% of individuals with autism exhibit symptoms of ADHD, and that up to 60% of individuals with ADHD exhibit symptoms of ASD. This means that there is a substantial possibility that an individual with ADHD could also have autism.

---

16 Baker, L. & Cantwell, D.P. (1992). Attention deficit disorder and speech/language disorders. *Comprehensive Mental Health Care*, 2(1), 3-16.

Tourette's Syndrome

Tourette's Syndrome in children with ADHD was once thought to be caused by stimulant medication; however, we now know that this is not the case. Recent research has shown that the two disorders have similar risk factors — smoking during pregnancy, being born prematurely, and low birth weight. Individuals with Tourette's Syndrome exhibit motor and vocal tics — rapid, repetitive movements and sounds. Less than 10% of individuals with ADHD have Tourette's Syndrome; however, around 70% of children with Tourette's Syndrome also have ADHD.

Oppositional Defiant Disorder (ODD)

Oppositional Defiant Disorder is the term used to describe a pattern of behaviours that includes a child losing their temper frequently, defying adult authority, refusing to cooperate, being easily annoyed and deliberately annoying others. In essence, these children display a 'counter- will' against authority, especially when frustrated or stressed. They are often completely inflexible in such situations, and the more pressure applied to make them conform the greater the opposition. They may say things like "you can't make me", "it's not fair" and "get out of my face or I will sue you".

The causes of ODD are hard to detect, but often there will be a pattern of frustration and intolerance as a result of a range of issues. These could include learning needs such as dyslexia, or behavioural needs such as unrecognised ADHD. Other reasons could be attachment problems in early childhood, low achievement and associated low self-esteem, lack of structure or a combination of these factors.

Over 5% of children have ODD. It is more common in young boys than young girls, but as age increases the ratio levels out. ODD is diagnosed in the same way as many other childhood psychiatric disorders, via a multi-modal assessment including a review of the family and medical history.

Conduct Disorder

Conduct Disorder is a type of behavioural difficulty where pupils often bully and show aggression to others. The key elements that describe Conduct Disorder are aggression to people or animals, destruction of property, deceitfulness and/or theft, and serious violations of rules. The difference between children with Conduct Disorder and ADHD is mainly one of 'wilful intent'. A child with Conduct Disorder is likely to be premeditated in his or her actions, and to have an alibi for every situation. In contrast, any thinking-through by a child with ADHD often comes too late – as he or she has already carried out the problematic action.

The causes of Conduct Disorder are uncertain, as there are many factors to consider. An important issue may be that of role models: children with Conduct Disorder often lack good role models and take their lead from inappropriate models of behaviour. It is more common for boys with Conduct Disorder to continue into adulthood with these types of problems than girls, who more often end up having mood and anxiety disorders as they mature. Substance abuse is very high among youngsters in this group: 60% of ten-year-olds with conduct disorder will be abusing substances four years later.

Mood Disorders

Mood disorders are a group of conditions that negatively affect a person's emotional state. They include relatively well-known issues such as clinical depression. Mood disorders and ADHD share symptoms such as inattention, sleep problems, feelings of sadness and lack of motivation. However, the causes of these symptoms are different across the two conditions. For example, individuals with ADHD may lack motivation because they feel overwhelmed, while individuals with a mood disorder may simply have a diminished drive to do anything at all.

People with ADHD are three times more likely to develop a mood disorder than the general population. Some experts hypothesize that as many as 70% of those with ADHD will be treated at some point in their lives for primary depression – either as a standalone illness, or for secondary depression caused by the experience of living with ADHD.

Bipolar Disorder

Bipolar disorder is a mood disorder characterized by mood swings – high periods of euphoria (mania) and low periods of depression – each lasting for weeks at a time. The high state is sometimes seen as hyperactivity and the low state as inattention and/or lack of motivation, all of which are common symptoms of ADHD. Thus, it can sometimes be a challenge to separate the two conditions. Up to 20% of individuals with ADHD also have bipolar disorder.

Anxiety Disorders

Anxiety disorders are characterised by feelings of intense worry, fear or unease. This group of disorders includes conditions such as phobias, obsessive-compulsive disorder (OCD) and post-traumatic stress disorder (PTSD). As is also the case with mood disorders, it is normal to experience these feelings at appropriate times and it is only when the problem interferes with functioning in daily life that help should be sought.

There are many possible causes of anxiety, ranging from physical conditions such as cardiac arrhythmias through to emotional reactions like excessive stress.

Up to 30% of people with ADHD also have an anxiety disorder. As with depression, the two share some common symptoms, such as a lack of focus, feelings of fearfulness and insomnia.

Sensory Processing Disorder (SPD)

Sensory processing disorder (SPD) is an inability to sort out external stimuli – making the smallest stimulus unbearable – or the need to search out high-stimulus activities to arouse sluggish senses. For most people, sensory processing develops normally through childhood; however, for some it does not develop as well as it should and causes problems with social participation, education and daily life. When researchers looked at children who showed symptoms of ADHD or SPD, up to 60% had symptoms of both disorders. Early, effective intervention is important in both cases. Occupational therapists are the professionals who typically evaluate for sensory processing disorder.

Specific Learning Difficulties (SpLD)

ADHD impacts behaviour and learning, but this is not the same thing as having a Specific Learning Difficulty (SpLD). As we noted in Chapter 1, SpLDs include dyslexia, developmental coordination disorder (dyspraxia) and dyscalculia. They are sometimes called Learning Disabilities, although this term can be confusing as it is also applied to individuals with more serious lifelong conditions like Down Syndrome.

Specific Learning Difficulties impact up to 50% of children with ADHD, compared to only 5% of children without ADHD. Those with a SpLD may have trouble organising thoughts, finding the right words to use when speaking, or remembering lessons. Reading and mathematics are most commonly affected. 12% of children with ADHD also have a co-existing speech disorder.

Ten key things to know about ADHD

1. ADHD stands for 'Attention Deficit Hyperactivity Disorder'.

2. It is a highly complex neurological condition with no single cause.

3. The core symptoms are inattention, hyperactivity and impulsivity.

4. Children with ADHD display 'consistent inconsistency' and can find it hard to shift gears.

5. The condition has formerly been referred to as 'Hyperkinetic Impulse Disorder' (HID) and 'Attention Deficit Disorder' (ADD).

6. It usually develops by the age of five, and it affects 3-9% of school aged children.

7. ADHD affects three times as many boys as girls, although girls may be underdiagnosed.

8. Overlap with other conditions is the norm, not the exception.

9. Assessment should be a multimodal discipline involving multiple sources and steps.

10. Effective treatment can lead to significant improvement in symptoms and outcomes.

Part 2: Learning and school

Chapter 5: Why do they look bored?

Well, the most likely answer to this question is: because they are.

Boredom is a fact of human life, but it is seldom talked about in schools. Teachers as a group often appear to be afraid of the term, and/or take it personally when someone says that they are bored. However, the truth is that boredom is a real feeling and it can affect people in a range of different ways, especially if they are bored a great deal of the time.

Key Point

Boredom is a real feeling and it can affect people in a range of different ways, especially if they are bored a great deal of the time.

There are two main potential reasons why someone in a classroom environment could be bored:

1. Because they cannot access the information owing to a processing issue.
2. Because they are genuinely unable to be interested in what they are being asked to do.

Looking at the first reason, if an individual is not at the same developmental level as their peers then they are likely to stand out in some way – and, in many cases, this will manifest itself as appearing bored. Boredom due to difficulties with processing the curriculum could be due to a wide range of factors including reading, spelling, hearing or visual issues. This should be addressed by undergoing assessment for any or all of these potential problems, and thereafter supporting each specific need identified.

Turning to the second reason, we must first accept that boredom is a real phenomenon and then consider in practice how to convert this boredome into interest – in other words, how to change the behaviour. One way would be to investigate the opposite of boredom, which could entail a list of words such as 'interested', 'variety' and 'stimulated'.

Throughout many years teaching and training in the field of ADHD, the authors have developed a process of reducing boredom through interest, variety and stimulation. We call this 'the Seven Ms', standing for Mindset, Mood, Motivation, Movement, Mindfulness, Medication and Memory. We will look at the first four in this chapter, and the last three in Chapter 6.

Mindset

It is hard to trace the origins of the word 'mindset', but some sources say it has been around since the 1920s. However, Stanford University psychologist Carol Dweck popularised the term when she went mainstream with her 2012 book, *Mindset: The New Psychology of Success*[17]. Dweck describes two different mindsets: a 'fixed mindset' and a 'growth mindset'.

In a **fixed mindset**, people believe that basic qualities such as intelligence or talent are simply fixed traits. They spend their time documenting their intelligence or talent instead of developing them. They also believe that talent alone creates success without effort, which Dweck believes is wrong.

In a **growth mindset**, people believe that their most basic abilities can be developed through dedication and hard work. In this scenario, brains and talent are just the starting point for growth. This view creates a love of learning and a resilience that is essential for great accomplishment.

Expert View

"Teaching a growth mindset creates motivation and productivity in the worlds of business, education, and sports. It enhances relationships."

Carol Dweck

In a school environment, some students are battered and bruised by the system and we need to teach them about a growth mindset – in other words, that nothing is fixed, that everything is fluid and that, in terms of learning, effort is much more important than achievement.

Mood

When it comes to reducing boredom and supporting attention as a teacher, there are three moods we need to be careful to manage.

The first is our own mood. In a good mood, we can handle most people. However, if before we even enter the classroom we've had a difficult journey into school or we aren't feeling well, then what might normally be little irritations can result in serious annoyance – especially if faced with a specific student that we don't really 'click' with. Also some students may sense that we are not at our best and pick away just to stir things up.

The second mood to manage is that of tricky individuals in the class. Can we read their mood when they first come in? Has their previous lesson been difficult, or are they really not ready to learn? Do they need some

---

17 Dweck, C.S. (2006). *Mindset: The new psychology of success.* New York: Random House.

time to settle? Have they had enough sleep the night before? Can we detect any friction between particular individuals coming into the room?

Finally, take another look at the 'players' in the class – those pupils who, if they become easily bored, are likely to wind up the more 'incendiary' individuals simply because this will be a source of entertainment for them.

So, instead of thinking about behaviour management, try to think about managing moods. The result will be a reduction in boredom and an improvement in class attention levels.

Motivation

The psychiatrist and theorist William Glasser[18] identified five core components of 'motivation' as follows: survival, belonging, power, freedom and fun. How we interpret these is crucial to classroom success. For the purpose of our model we shall overlook 'survival' (as schools are generally secure places for young people) and 'freedom' (as while there are choices to be made as a pupil moves up the school, many decisions are 'hardwired' as part of educational policy).

In terms of 'belonging', every student must feel that they are an integral part of their class. They should value their time in the classroom and, above all, all feel valued by their teacher. As for 'power', every individual should feel that they have the status and opportunity to present their skills in ways that add value to the overall class dynamics, whether that be presenting learning knowledge themselves or helping others to learn.

Finally we should remember that, young or old, everybody likes to have 'fun'. So let's make the whole experience of learning fun and mix up the format once in a while; play games and quizzes, promote role play, and make creative use of ICT to present information or review learning.

Movement

It's truly astonishing that, in today's world, the dominant model for formal learning remains 'sit still'. Why do we persist with this when the evidence that lecturing alone does not suffice is so compelling?[19,20]

18 Glasser, W. (1999). *Choice Theory*. New York: HarperPerennial.

19 Dolcourt J.L. (2000). Commitment to change: a strategy for promoting educational effectiveness. *Journal of Continuing Education in the Health Professions*. 20: 156-63.

20 Slavin, R.E. (1994). *Educational Psychology: Theory into Practice*. 4th ed. Boston: Allyn and Bacon.

The reason for the gap between what we know and what we do can be traced back more than a century. For decades, the educational and scientific communities seemed to believe that thinking was thinking and movement was movement, and each was as separate as could be. The truth is that movement can strengthen learning, improve memory and enhance learner motivation and morale, and most neuroscientists now agree that movement and cognition are powerfully connected.

The brain area most associated with motor control is the cerebellum. This is located at the back of the brain, just under the occipital lobe, and it is about the size of a small fist. The cerebellum takes up just one-tenth of the brain by volume, but contains nearly half of all its neurons.[21]

Many teachers know about the link between learning and movement; however, just as many dismiss it once children get beyond the first two years of school. Yet the relationship between movement and learning is so strong that it pervades all aspects of life – and emotions are intertwined in the mix as well. Teachers still generally consign movement, emotion and thinking to separate 'compartments'. As a result, pupils may feel awkward if they want to express emotions or move around when teachers want them to stay still and think. Instead teachers need to realise that what the students are experiencing is simply a healthy integration of mind and body.

Many teachers have found that programmes incorporating movement can help learners with SEND (Special Educational Needs and Disabilities). Some of these learners are stuck in counterproductive mental states, and movement is a quick way to change them. More generally, movement – such as that involved in playing active games – activates the brain across a wide variety of areas. It may be the stimulation of such neural networks that helps trigger some learning. For other students, the rise in energy and increased blood flow may put them in a better mood to think and recall. Some routines that call for slower movement can do the reverse, calming students who are overactive and supporting a state of concentration.

As a result of all this, teachers should purposefully integrate movement activities into everyday learning; not just hands-on classroom activities, but also daily stretching, walks, dance, drama, seat-changing, energisers, and physical education. Below are some examples of easy-to-use strategies.

---

21   Ivry, R.B., & Fiez, J.A. (2000). Cerebellar contributions to cognition and imagery. In M.S. Gazzaniga (Ed.), *The new cognitive neurosciences* (2nd ed). Cambridge, MA: MIT Press.

How to help – integrating movement with learning

☞ **Goal-setting on the move.** Start each class with an activity in which everyone pairs up. Students can mime their goals or convey them by playing charades, or the pairs can go for a short walk while setting goals. Ask students to answer three focusing questions, such as those listed below. You can also invent other questions or ask students to create some of their own.

- What are my goals for today and this week?
- What must I do today and this week in this class to reach my goals?
- Why is it important for me to reach my goals today?

☞ **Drama and role plays.** Get the class used to daily or at least weekly role plays. Have pupils play charades to review important ideas. Do one-minute commercials adapted from television to advertise upcoming content or to review past content.

☞ **Quick games.** Use ball-toss games for review, vocabulary-building, storytelling or self-disclosure. Have students rewrite lyrics to familiar songs in pairs or as a team. The new words can provide a content review. Then have the students perform the song with choreography.

☞ **Stretching.** To open class, or anytime that you and your pupils need more oxygen, get everyone up to do some slow stretching. Ask pupils to lead the whole group, or let teams do their own stretching. Allow learners more mobility in the classroom during specific times. Give them errands to do, make a jump rope available, or let them walk around the back of the classroom as long as they do not disturb others.

☞ **Breaktimes.** Teachers should also ensure that breaktimes include some movement – no standing around all the time!

Chapter 6: How can I engage their interest?

In Chapter 5, we introduced the 'Seven Ms' approach to reducing boredom among pupils and explored Mindset, Mood, Motivation and Movement. This chapter looks at the final three Ms: Mindfulness, Medication and Memory.

Mindfulness

Most teacher training focuses primarily on content and pedagogy, overlooking the very real social, emotional and cognitive demands of classroom teaching itself. Mindfulness is a process that allows one to stay focused on the present moment and, through non-judgmental awareness, it can help to promote the calm, relaxed and enlivened environment that children need to learn. Mindfulness can also help us to become more effective at managing mood, reducing conflict and developing more positive ways of relating in the classroom. Below we explore three ways in which developing skill in mindfulness techniques can help us to become better teachers (and parents!).

Key Point

Mindfulness allows one to stay focused on the present moment and can help to promote the environment that children need to learn.

Understanding our own emotions

When teaching, our minds are often so focused on what we need to do that we fail to pay attention to the present moment. This can generate unhelpful expectations about how things ought to be and we can become attached to them, rather than noticing and accepting how things really are. If this happens it can lead to distress, affecting our perceptions and making us more sensitive to threat.

For example, we may imagine that a student's disruptive behavior is intentionally designed to interfere with the teaching when in fact it is the normal behaviour of a child who needs help with self-regulation. If we take this behaviour personally, we may lose our temper and say something that makes matters worse. Practising mindfulness can help us as teachers to recognise our emotional patterns and proactively regulate how we behave, responding in the way we want to rather than reacting automatically.

Communicating more effectively

There is a mistaken belief among many teachers that they can and must control pupils' behaviour. This sets the stage for power struggles, in which attempts to exert control are likely to backfire. It's far better to create and maintain an effective learning environment by learning to control oneself. We can control how we communicate, how we behave and where we position our bodies in space. We can set and reinforce expectations and limits, and we can control the physical space so that it supports learning.

Knowing what's going on in the classroom and with students is critical to the ability to orchestrate the social-emotional dynamics and manage the physical spaces that are conducive to learning. Practising mindful awareness helps us develop the skill of paying attention in the present moment and learning to see what's truly happening in our classroom, allowing us to devise better solutions to the problems we see before us.

Managing pace

Sometimes as new teachers we can be too intent on getting through the lesson plans and unconsciously start to rush. Slowing down and deliberately pausing for a moment of mindfulness can give us time to ask ourselves how we are feeling, what's happening in the classroom, and what our students need at that particular moment. It also models mindfulness for students.

The speed at which students process information varies. Some process auditory information very quickly, while others tend to have more visual or sensorimotor strengths. Younger children require more time to process than older children, though adults often forget this. No matter what their age, students process information better when they are given a little extra time, and consciously creating pauses throughout a lesson helps support this.

Too often teachers forget to pause after asking a question, or interrupt student hesitations, not giving them a chance to think through their answers. Pausing is helpful during lecturing to give students time to absorb information and consolidate thinking, and during student work periods to give them uninterrupted time to figure things out for themselves. It can also generate feelings of suspense and expectation, enlivening the classroom.

Medication

As we have already seen, ADHD is the umbrella term given to describe a wide range of attention difficulties, which we now know result from a neurobiological difference in brain chemistry due to dopamine and noradrenaline not working in a typical manner. One method of supporting this is the use of chemical stimulants to help young people with attention and focus. We will not spend time on this topic here, but we will explore the use of medication in greater detail in Part 4.

Memory

Many students have problems with memory. These can be subdivided into those who have problems with short-term and/or working memory (these are closely related, but we will look at the suble differences in Chapter 8), and those who have problems with the operation of long-term memory.

Individuals who have deficits in registering information in short-term memory often have difficulty remembering instructions or directions, remembering what has just been said during conversations and class discussions, and remembering what they have just read. Such students also often forget what they are doing while they are doing it.

Students who have deficits in the storage and retrieval of information from long-term memory may study hard for tests, but not be able to recall the information they studied when the test takes place. They frequently have difficulty recalling specific factual information such as dates or grammatical rules, and have a poor memory of material previously learned. They may also be unable to answer specific questions asked of them in class, even when their parents and/or teachers believe that they do know the answer.

Below are some strategies to help young people develop a more efficient and effective memory.

H2h How to help – memory support techniques

☞ **Many formats.** Students can benefit from being given directions in both verbal and visual formats. In addition, a student's understanding and memorising of instructions can be checked by encouraging them to repeat the directions and explain their meaning. Giving examples of what needs to be done can also often helpful for enhancing memory.

☞ **Overlearning.** Students should be taught the necessity of 'overlearning' new information. Often they practise only until they are able to perform one error-free repetition of the material. However, several error-free repetitions are necessary to solidify the information.

☞ **Using cues.** According to research, information is more easily retrieved from memory when it is stored using a cue – and that cue should be present at the time the information is being retrieved. For example, the acronym HOMES can be used to represent the names of the Great Lakes: Huron, Ontario, Michigan, Erie and Superior. The acronym is a cue that is used when the information is being learnt, and recalling the cue when taking a test will help the student to recall the information.

☞ **Word substitution.** This cue strategy can be used for information that is hard to visualise. Such information can be converted into words that sound familiar and are more easily visualised. For example, the word 'occipital' can be converted to 'exhibit hall' (because it sounds similar). The student can then make a visual image of walking into an art gallery and seeing a big painting of a brain with big bulging eyes (the occipital region of the brain controls vision). With this system, the vocabulary word the student is trying to remember actually becomes the cue for the visual image that then cues the definition of the word.

☞ **Note taking.** To enhance short-term memory when reading, students should underline, highlight, or jot key words in the margin. They can then go back and look at these notes. To consolidate this information in long-term memory, they can make outlines or use graphic organisers (research shows that these can increase academic achievement for all students). Students who have a short-term memory weakness should write down each step rather than relying on mental arithmetic when solving maths problems, and should keep a piece of paper to hand to jot down notes and prevent them forgetting what they are doing.

☞ **Retrieval practice.** Research has shown that long-term memory is enhanced when students engage in retrieval practice. Taking a test is a retrieval practice, i.e. the act of recalling information that has been studied from long-term memory. Thus, it can be helpful for students to take practice tests. When teachers are reviewing information prior to tests and exams, they could ask the students questions or have the students make up questions for everyone to answer rather than just re-teaching the same information. Also, if students are required or encouraged to make up their own tests and take them, it will give their parents and/or teachers information about whether they really know the key information or are focusing on details that are less important.

Chapter 7: How can I create a class that is ready to learn?

To create a fully inclusive classroom is a huge undertaking for overstretched, overwhelmed teachers in our mainstream schools – juggling assessment deadlines, rewriting curriculum statements, subject leadership staff meetings, attempting assessment without levels, playground duty cover and a temperamental photocopier can seem like an unachievable mountain to climb, and this may be just on Monday morning! And all this while we are also being told to promote our own wellbeing and work-life balance!

Today's mainstream classrooms comprise a diverse range of children, all with different strengths, interests, needs, skills and challenges – some of which will not yet have been identified. A class can have children with the same diagnosis who present in completely different ways; or, in contrast, children with quite different diagnoses who present with similar challenges and barriers. A strategy that is successful for one child may not be effective for another, or may only be effective for a short period of time.

Key Point

Today's mainstream classrooms comprise a diverse range of children, all with different strengths, interests, needs, skills and challenges.

In light of these many challenges, it is vital that the moment a teacher walks into a classroom full of children their eyes, hearts, ears and minds are open to the carefully planned learning opportunities that will be delivered. Achieving this means creating an environment that is as inclusive as possible, which in turn means being fully aware of each individual young person's strengths and difficulties.

Who or what is the SENCO?

The *SEND Code of Practice: 0 to 25 years*[22] requires every educational setting to have a named SENCO in post. SENCO is an acronym for 'Special Educational Needs Coordinator'. It is worth noting that the role of the SENCO in schools has changed significantly over time since 1994, when

---

22 Department for Education and Department of Health and Social Care (2014) Special educational needs and disability code of practice: 0 to 25 years. Available at: https://www.gov.uk/government/publications/send-code-of-practice-0-to-25

the Code of Practice on the Identification and Assessment of Special Educational Needs was written. Then, the role of the SENCO was fairly operational, requiring an element of coordination and organisation. Over time, and through changes in legislative reviews, the role has become more managerial and strategic, with the 2015 code of practice stating that the SENCO 'should' be on the school leadership team. 'Should' is however not 'must', and this is not the case in all schools.

The SENCO, who is sometimes referred to as the Inclusion Manager, is a vital resource for class teachers to understand their students before they begin teaching them. Every child in the school, with or without a diagnosis, should be known to the SENCO, and a comprehensive handover makes initial planning far more achievable. In their strategic and managerial capacity, the SENCO will know the children in each class in a wide range of settings, situations and circumstances. They should be clear on how far they have come and where they are going next, and they should already have a well established relationship with the young person and the family.

The SENCO should always be a teacher's first port of call. Use them to find out what inspires and engages each student, what strengths they have, what teaching strategies have worked in the past, what motivates them, who they work best with and what should be in place to support them. The SENCO should have a deep and broad knowledge of each and every student, and they may therefore be able to help you to see things with a wider and more strategic perspective. Forewarned is forearmed!

Making effective use of Teaching Assistants (TAs) and other adults

If you are fortunate enough to have additional adults within your classroom, use them wisely to ensure that they have a purposeful role across elements of your lesson – whether it be during whole class delivery, during small group work or assisting on an individual basis. Possible effective uses of an additional adult to support children with attention difficulties could be:

- Re-prompting attention and focus to a vulnerable student during whole class teaching.
- Pre-teaching key vocabulary before a lesson to support a student in accessing what will be delivered.
- Adding visual aids or notes to a whiteboard beside a child while the teacher is talking – presenting what is being discussed in a visual way.

- Providing small sensory breaks to a child who may be distracted and sensory seeking and therefore missing teacher delivery; this could be as simple as firmly resting their hands on the child's shoulders.

- Cueing a learner to visual aids in the room that are being indicated. A child struggling with attention may only be processing one sensory input at a time, so if they are listening, they may well not be looking!

- Chunking up learning for a child, in order to give them only one or two instructions at a time and avoid overload.

- Asking a child to repeat back verbally given information so as to embed it into long term memory.

- Building a task board that a child can access and manage independently, with visual cues for each stage of the learning that will be delivered.

It is vital that supporting adults in the classroom are clear as to their role during all parts of a lesson in order to be effective. Supporting adults aren't extra pupils for you to manage; used effectively, they are an invaluable resource for the teacher seeking inclusivity. So use them as a tool to engage, not as a crutch (it can be easy for a child to become too reliant on adult help), and experiment with the relationships between adults and pupils to find the right balance of support and independence for each young person.

Are your materials accessible?

Careful differentiation of the written materials that you provide to the children in your class is vital to support them in being able to access what you are delivering. Often, children with attention difficulties will be reading at a lower age level than their neurotypical peers. For example:

- Dyslexic children will find decoding skills a challenge.
- Children with language delay may find reading comprehension difficult.
- Children with ASD may have challenges with the inference of read texts.
- Children with ADHD may have delayed acquisition of reading skills as they struggle to attend to task, and thus have gaps in previous learning.

All these children in your classroom may be demonstrating their individual needs with some attention difficulties, so ensuring that written materials are accessible and at the appropriate level will create a supportive environment rather than an additional barrier when they do attend to task. Use of images to go alongside the written word are vital to support understanding, and to provide an alternative way in for children who find decoding difficult.

H2h How to help – creating an inclusive classroom

☞ **Know your starting point.** Make sure that you are clear on the starting points and entry assessment data for every student in your class. Read historic paperwork, diagnosis documents if any are available and previous reviewed plans and reports. Knowing a child's starting point from a data perspective, as well as any diagnosis or assessments that have taken place, is vital to ensure that you are fully prepared.

☞ **Keep an open mind.** It is too easy to let a diagnosis define a child. Consider a diagnosis not as a label but as a list of ingredients, within which every child is different. It is important not to 'clump' children with correlating diagnoses together for this reason. Many children spend so long on the pathway to a diagnosis that it can seem like the end of the road – the answer to the problem. However, a diagnosis doesn't signpost the teacher or parent to the next road on the map – one that will enlighten the child and support him or her to be happy and learn. It is therefore vital to consider the diagnosis as a milestone on the journey rather than the final destination.

☞ **Maintain a dialogue with colleagues.** In a primary setting, speak to the previous class teacher. What worked? What made things harder for her? What motivated him? Speak to the other adults around the school and find out what their focus and attention is like in other areas of your setting. How is lunchtime? What about PE? By establishing which lessons or parts of the day are more successful, you can consider how to mirror that supportive environment into the parts of the day that are proving more challenging. Draw on your colleagues' wealth of knowledge, views and experiences to build solutions together.

☞ **Begin with the need, not the diagnosis.** A diagnosis of ADHD, ASD, dyslexia, attachment, trauma or any other difficulty that a child with attention difficulties may have does not necessarily make a difference to their needs in your classroom. All these children may have poor focus, poor self-organisation, poor memory skills and word finding difficulties; all may be easily distracted, struggle with sensory overload, suffer with poor self-esteem and find peer relationships difficult. Be it one or all of these challenges, the child in your classroom may find attending to your lesson difficult without supportive measures in place.

☞ **Look past the label at the whole child.** It is important to consider each student's abilities as well as their needs. Try to see each individual as a whole child, with strengths and difficulties, and ask yourself what advantages their needs bring to the table. For example, a child diagnosed with ADHD who struggles to give you their full attention may be curious, energetic, think outside the box and be persistent. A child diagnosed with ASD may struggle to process verbal instructions but have significant attention to detail, excellent visual memory skills, resistance to peer pressure and a logical approach to problem solving. A dyslexic child who finds the recall of instructions a challenge could also be incredibly creative, have excellent spatial understanding, be skilled in reading people and have strong verbal communication skills.

☞ **Keep your own growth mindset.** When faced with a child who cannot attend to your carefully planned task, ask yourself "How can I change how I deliver this so she can remember?" or "What is the next stage in this learning journey?" Keeping the power of 'yet' to end a statement opens the door for a fresh start and new approach tomorrow!

☞ **Keep your class, a class!** Try to avoid removing individual pupils for support or interventions during lessons. Sometimes this cannot be avoided; however, maintaining a cohesive class community is important for all children, particularly those with diverse needs that present as attention difficulties. These students are particularly vulnerable to delicate self-esteem, poor peer relationships and a lack of belonging; all of which are vital for them to 'buy in' to your rules, expectations and routines. Additionally, taking a child out of class who already finds attention, focus and recall a challenge will only result in them missing even more of your valuable teaching. Maintain a sense of community, with everyone playing their part, as best you can.

Get to know your learners outside the classroom. Building a culture of trust and mutual respect is a powerful and effective way to support your most vulnerable learners. By involving yourself in the wider school day – after school clubs, lunch in the hall, on the playground before first bell, school trips – you and your learners gain opportunities to see each other in alternative settings and to build stronger relationships. This will increase the probability of successful learning.

 Ask for help! Even experienced SENCOs don't know everything, and we are all learning every day. Each child is different and new research is carried out all the time. So draw on available resources – listen to parents, learn from experienced professionals speaking in multi-agency meetings, and chat with colleagues such as Speech and Language Therapists, Community Paediatricians, Nurture Workers, Counsellors, Social Workers, Specialist teachers and Educational Psychologists. Read that book, ask to go on that course and keep learning every day!

Chapter 8: Why can't they remember?

The three words "I can't remember" are uttered in a million schools and homes around the country and the world every day. In a classroom environment, these words are much more likely to be spoken by a child with attention difficulties than by a neurotypical child. They can lead to frustration for the well-prepared teacher following a carefully planned lesson input – as well as for the child with attention difficulties, who cannot remember what has just been said or what they need to do to follow instructions and be successful in your lesson, no matter how hard they try.

What is memory and how does it work?

Memory is the brain's ability to understand, encode, organise, store and recall information. Without a fully functioning memory, we would lack the ability to remember past thoughts and experiences or previously learned facts and skills. Acquiring the ability to do this – and to make links between these areas – is a key part of cognitive development and learning.

Memory is composed of many factors. Short term and working memory contribute to the brain's executive functioning capacity, which then works to send information to our long term memory storage. However, before memory ever comes into play, attention is a critical aspect. Simply put, attention funnels the information we need to know into our brains. And, for children with attention difficulties, this is the first challenge.

Assuming our attention has functioned as it should, once information has been gathered and sent to the brain it is fed into our short term memory. This part of the brain, within the prefrontal cortex, coordinates immediate facts and is not fully developed until the age of fifteen. Research varies in its judgment of the capacity of working memory, with some studies showing that the average short term memory can hold up to seven[23] items for a minute and others that the limit is four items for fifteen seconds.[24]

Once information is in our short term memory, it is the role of our working memory to manipulate it so that it is useful. This is an instant process that, once complete, sends organised information into our long term memory storage facility. Until relatively recently, the terms 'short term memory' and 'working memory' were used fairly interchangeably. However, recently it has been shown that they have very different roles.[25] People with ADHD are often described as having a poor short-term memory; however, researchers have noted that the children with ADHD they studied displayed sound short term memory skills.[26] Only after the information left the short term memory did an impairment become clear. Children with ADHD can often recall what has just been said, or repeat back a verbal instruction – however, taking that information forward to the next stage of learning is where the challenge lies.

In a child with working memory difficulties the long term memory storage facility is often disorganised, with information incorrectly stored, not carrying so much relevant and useful meaning, or even lost altogether on its way in. As students with ADHD struggle with impaired attention and also impaired working memory, it is important that we develop alternative strategies and support to develop these areas if we are to help them remember, and ultimately enable them to achieve success within the classroom.

23 Miller, G. (1956). The magical number seven, plus or minus two: Some limits on our capacity for processing information. *The psychological review*, 63, 81-97.

24 Cowan N. (2001). The magical number four in short-term memory: a reconsideration of mental storage capacity. *Behavioral and Brain Sciences* 24, 87–114.

25 Aben, B., Stapert, S., & Blokland, A. (2012). About the distinction between working memory and short-term memory. *Frontiers in Psychology*, 3, Article 301.

26 Alloway, T., (2016). What is the link between ADHD and working memory? *Psychology Today*, 27 June 2016

H2h How to help – reducing working memory overload

☞ Ensure that the length of the activities is considered. Long tasks requiring multiple steps for success can mean that a child with working memory challenges will be less likely to complete the task successfully.

☞ Consider the relevance and importance of the information that is being captured and attended to for students. Classrooms are often filled with verbal information that is not required, mixed with important information. Ensure when talking to the class that you keep verbal information precise and useful, without too much unnecessary dialogue. For example, talking to one child about their upcoming music lesson in front of the whole class can add to short term memory pressures for a child with ADHD, as their brain tries to process this and decide it is not important, As a result, another learning opportunity may be lost.

☞ Where possible, try to deliver information that is meaningful and draws on previous knowledge. Cue the students into this link as it may not come naturally. For example, telling a child that the rules for Hockey that we are already secure about will help us to understand the game rules for a new sport of Lacrosse, can support activation of a background switch for children and lessen the pressure on their brain to do so.

☞ Be aware of simplifying pressures on mental processing. If we are providing a child with new information that must be processed and stored, we must be mindful to not also expect them to mentally process or do something with this information before it is securely stored. For example, when teaching a new spelling pattern, try to wait for it to have been stored, with patterns, visual aids and practice, before asking the brain to mentally process this and use it when spelling a new word.

☞ Try to make sure that your instructions are concise, and ask students to repeat these back to you while a peer makes notes to support their remembering. Asking the whole class to repeat back to you chorally, or to answer a question in unison, can be a powerful adjustment to support children with working memory challenges.

Our brains are wired to utilise patterning as a tool for long term memory storage. When our brain attends to an input, our working memory scans our long term memory for previous experience of this and any similar patterns. We can support patterning when children are learning new information by using mnemonics (for example, 'Never Eat Shredded Wheat' for compass directions), by utilising songs or music (for example, rapping instructions or singing times tables to nursery rhymes) and by chunking instructions (breaking them into small chunks so students can process each chunk while avoiding overload and shutdown).

Chapter 9: How can I support them to recall information?

In the 1940s, American educator Edgar Dale introduced the 'cone of experience' model in order to suggest the relative concreteness of the learning resulting from various kinds of stimuli.[27] While the specific numbers widely attached to this research (and shown below) were actually introduced later by others, and Dale himself declared that his approach was not intended to be rigorously scientific, his work provides a useful benchmark for thinking about levels of recall and understanding as we move from passive learning to active participation. According to Dale and those who followed him, passive verbal information results in low levels of recall, while active participation results in high engagement and much more effective levels of recall.

It is often stated that we remember:

- 10% of what we read
- 20% of what we hear
- 30% of what we see
- 50% of what we see and hear
- 70% of what we say and discuss with others
- 80% of what we experience
- 90% of what we teach by doing and saying

Let the child become the teacher

With the above ideas in mind, adaptations to more active models of classroom teaching and learning can embrace the notion that children themselves can become teachers. Creating a culture of partner work is one way to do this, with clear teacher and student roles that rotate regularly and fairly within each partnership. Drawing on other year groups is another strategy – making use of a 'buddy' system, with older children supporting reading or teaching mathematical models to their younger peers.

---

27 Dale, E. (1946). *Audio-Visual Methods in Teaching*. New York: Dryden Press.

Perhaps most effective of all, having students literally teach material provides clear and measurable outcomes to learning experiences. Can a student research a historical event with a view to teaching the class what they find out, and in doing so move from the 10% success rate of learning what is read to the 90% success rate of learning what is taught to others?

Develop visualisation skills

Visualisation means to create an image of something in your brain – to see it there. This can be beneficial for a young person with working memory challenges, as it uses the visual-spatial element of working memory to add another layer to the information stored. If you ask a child with ADHD to collect their exercise book, ruler, pencil and eraser verbally, they may well get to their table and call out "What did I need?" as their working memory has lost the information. Asking the same child to picture in their head what they need, and where on their desk they will put it, adds another layer to the stored information and can support the memory function.

Memory is enhanced by drama – bright colours, evocative smells, exciting action and heightened emotion. This can be as simple as making a child laugh when creating a visual pictoword, or providing a cartoon version of a word's meaning. Or, when asking a child to collect resources around the classroom, they could be asked to visualise, or imagine, collecting each item on the way to their table, or to create a quick map of the route that they will take. These simple techniques can support the storage of the key information that is required to be remembered.

Visualisation is also key in developing reading comprehension skills. For a child to fully comprehend what has been read and move to the deeper levels of inference and deduction, a clear visual map of the words that have been decoded must be in place. For children with working memory challenges, once a text has been decoded or said out loud the active process of reading is complete. Ensure your students know that in order to be a successful reader, they must in addition be visualising what they have read. Encourage them to physically draw a story snapshot. This can then lead to probing and pertinent questioning, and teach the deeper layer of reading understanding.

How to help – encouraging visual memory

Human beings are intrinsically built to respond to what they see. Ensuring that a classroom is clear and well-structured can not only help children who find being organised a challenge, but also support their memory processing with visual cues. Ensure that expectations are visually modelled and children are 'shown' what to do – remembering that students with impaired working memory may need access to this visual aid for longer, and may need to revisit it more regularly, than their neurotypical peers.

☞ Ensure that organised areas are clearly labelled with visual prompts as well as words – for example, label trays and cupboards with words and an image of what is stored there.

☞ Use word mats and/or word banks, again with visual prompts. These may be organised alphabetically or colour coded by word type. Pre-teaching vocabulary with a clear model of how to use the word bank can be a useful strategy.

☞ Modelled and scaffolded writing – remember that those children with attention impairments will need longer access to material on the class board, as well as managing the distraction of the rest of the classroom. It can be effective to allow a child to use technology, such as a tablet, to photograph the modelled writing or calculation from the board, and to keep this on their table to refer to throughout the lesson.

☞ Use visual timetables to support organisation of the school day, or a visual task board to organise a lesson's structure and available resources. This can provide children with a reliable source of support that also moves them towards independence and self-management.

Muscle memory and multisensory learning

Repetition, or 'doing' something repeatedly, is key to strengthening and building neural pathways and developing long term muscle memory. When we learn to ride a bike, or drive a car, this is a physical and kinaesthetic activity. We don't learn to ride a bike by someone telling us how it's done, and we can't learn to drive a car by reading a manual about it. We learn by doing and, as experienced drivers will know, the early days of rigid instructor control give way to getting from A to B while thinking about other things entirely. We are driving using muscle memory – our brains have followed these procedures so many times that it is no longer a working memory function, and instead long term muscle memory is in play.

Supporting children with ADHD in your classrooms to develop muscle memory will require them to 'do' your lesson, task or function, and to repeat its processes and activities, over and over, until the neural pathways are sufficiently established and secure that the brain no longer needs to work through the information each time. Repetition and rehearsal of information or processes support the journey of these concepts to the long term memory store, as "neurons that fire together, wire together."[28]

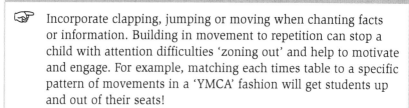

How to help – encouraging muscle memory

☞ Incorporate clapping, jumping or moving when chanting facts or information. Building in movement to repetition can stop a child with attention difficulties 'zoning out' and help to motivate and engage. For example, matching each times table to a specific pattern of movements in a 'YMCA' fashion will get students up and out of their seats!

☞ Race against the clock – ask students to write out a spelling or keyword repeatedly in a range of coloured pens against a sand timer – repeating tomorrow with a view to beating today's score!

☞ Use tapping or finger patterns when recalling a string of letters or numbers in order to build in a kinaesthetic link to the sequence.

---

28 Hebb, D.O. (1949). *The Organization of Behavior.* New York: John Wiley & Sons.

☞ For children who struggle with reversing the letters b and d, physically creating the word 'bed' with two clenched fists and index fingers as the bed's ascenders can be a useful tool.

☞ When learning spellings, we can connect visual, auditory and kinaesthetic processes by saying the spelling out loud (auditory) whilst air writing, tracing on the palm of our hand or drawing on a board or a tray of glitter, all of which are both physical and visual processes.

Do one thing at a time!

For many years, multitasking has been seen and promoted as the epitome of success and productivity. It is even cited as a strength in many job interviews! Yet multitasking comes with risks: we have all been guilty of trying to do too many things at once, like spinning plates in a circus fashion – hopping from one plate to the next and trying to prevent them all crashing to the ground!

Despite the apparent desirability of multitasking as a skill, a recent study shows that 'unitasking', or 'monotasking' – in plain language, 'doing one thing at a time' – actually results in greater levels of efficiency and higher quality outcomes over time . For the easily distracted students with ADHD in our classrooms, the tendency for their attention to wander can lead to inadvertent multitasking – which often leads to incomplete or inadequate outcomes as their attention and focus flits from one thing to another.

By promoting monotasking, we can channel the hyper focus that a child with ADHD intrinsically possesses and use it effectively to its full potential.

H2h How to help – encouraging monotasking

☞ Set time limits and use a visual reminder – for example a sand timer, or a countdown clock on the whiteboard. Setting a measurable time limit for a task or activity focuses attention onto this one thing.

☞ Provide one instruction at a time to allow each part or function to be completed before moving on to the next.

☞ Minimise external distractions: close the classroom door so that pupils are not distracted by the music lesson next door; lower the blinds so that the PE lesson outside doesn't become a focus.

☞ Ensure that motivating factors are in place – are the students motivated and excited by this task? See chapters 5 and 6 for more on this.

☞ Manage internal distractions; provide a notepad for students to jot anything that pops into their head to be dealt with later.

☞ Consider careful seating placement – a student will find it simpler to focus on one thing with minimised distractions. Sitting alongside a good role model, or at a solo workstation, can minimise external distractions.

Chapter 10: How can I help them to be organised?

In every class of schoolchildren there will be individuals who have difficulties with organisation. There will be those who never have the right equipment, constantly forget their P.E. bag or swimming kit and lose books, coats and letters home. Frustration leads us to use clichés; "You'd forget your head if it wasn't attached!" This disorganisation can be reflected in the work that these children do – it seems that their thoughts and ideas are as jumbled as their possessions, so that writing a sentence or solving a numeracy problem can be as daunting to them as remembering what lessons they have today.

Disorganisation can be a symptom of speech and language problems. A child's difficulty in understanding or interpreting instructions can make them appear disorganised because they aren't sure what they should be doing in an activity. They may miss important information like knowing what books they need and what activities they are expected to do for homework.

Disorganisation has been associated with Autism Spectrum Disorder, ADHD, Developmental Coordination Disorder (dyspraxia) and epilepsy amongst other conditions and, although children with these diagnoses are often disorganised, it is a trait common to many people – adults and children alike! Of course, it is assumed that children with special needs will be assessed by the relevant professionals and will have specific individual programmes developed for them. Small changes can make a big difference in the lives of your disorganised pupils and, by extension, in your life too.

We all have an idea of what it means to be disorganised, some of it from first hand experience! Most of us will have had times when we just couldn't find the car keys or forgot a dentist appointment. Of course, there are degrees of disorganisation – a spectrum which could have at one extreme a consistent state of disarray and confusion and, at the other, an occasional memory lapse. Some definitions encompass a whole raft of behaviours that can be associated with the label 'disorganised child'. Here are a few (taken from the website www.disorganisedchildren.org):

- Restricted coping strategies
- Doesn't learn from experience
- Patchy cognitive function
- Prefers structured activities
- Impaired short term memory
- Overloaded by complex stimuli
- Restlessness and poor attention span
- Fear of failure
- Reduced comprehension
- Inability to sequence data

The list goes on, and many of the items are included in the definitions we have for ADHD, Autism Spectrum Disorder, Developmental Coordination Disorder and Dyslexia. There is no doubt that disorganisation can be an aspect of all these special needs, but there is another side to it. Disorganisation is often associated with creativity and even genius – just look at those time-honoured images of the crazy professor or the actor with an 'artistic' personality, who may not be able to organise themselves but can come up with fantastic, original ideas or mesmerising performances!

There is a grain of truth in this but, despite these potentially positive aspects, there are many more drawbacks to disorganisation. This is especially true in schools, where children are expected to retain a large amount of information (both academic and practical) and, increasingly, to manage their own time and equipment. The positive aspect of dealing with disorganisation is that it is not an irreversible trait; it can be tackled with strategies that can be learned and practised. Moreover, there are tangible benefits in becoming more organised, some of which are listed here:

- **Organisation helps learning.** Children can think more clearly if their minds aren't occupied with secondary concerns, such as "Have I got the right worksheet?" If a student's work area is tidy and clear of irrelevant clutter, they are more able to concentrate on the task in hand and find the things that they need to complete it.
- **Organisation leads to improved time management.** Half a lesson can easily be wasted by a disorganised child hunting for mislaid equipment or finding out what they are supposed to be doing. When time is spent constructively in preparation, less time is wasted repeating tasks or worse, doing nothing.

- **Organisation improves self-esteem.** Children who feel in control of their immediate surroundings, who can find what they need and know what they are doing, tend to feel good about themselves. Increasing independence and confidence generally leads to higher self-esteem.

- **Being organised helps you fit in.** Most children in school manage their lives very well. If they didn't, there would be chaos! On the whole, children want to be like their peers and not singled out for negative attention, so a disorganised child can feel isolated, unpopular or simply embarrassed. A child who is organised, by contrast, will fit in and feel like one of the crowd.

- **Being organised helps you cope with school and enjoy life.** Children have a lot to deal with in school. They are learning about relationships with other children and adults (relationships that are not always positive), they are required to absorb and recall lots of information on demand, and they need to be able to organise themselves and their possessions. If they have problems with the latter, it will colour many aspects of their school life and make those other experiences even more difficult to deal with.

- **Being organised makes you feel safe and secure.** As mentioned above, children who have other special needs often experience organisational difficulties. Such children, and to a lesser extent all children, generally like to have an environment which feels safe and predictable, and which doesn't present them with stressful, unforeseen situations. Good organisational skills, either modelled by adults or taught directly, are vital in order to support these children so that they can begin to organise themselves.

Having established that being disorganised is not generally beneficial to the child, and that there are strategies that can be used to improve organisational skills, it is important that the teacher and supporting adults set a good example by demonstrating these skills in school. A well-organised classroom will help you and the children in your care to find books and equipment more easily, it will enable you to keep the classroom tidy and uncluttered, and it will create an environment conducive to learning that also feels secure and welcoming. In organising your classroom you should be attempting to create an ethos that promotes (amongst many other things):

- Consistency with regard to rules, rituals and routines.
- Flexibility in terms of understanding specific student needs.
- Structured movement to maintain positive mood and motivation.
- Questioning and discussion in learning.

- Relating learning to purpose both in the short term and long term.
- Role modelling and practising what you preach.
- Developing rapport and respect for others at all times.

In addition, a classroom should also be as inclusive as possible, so that all students can benefit from the learning environment. It's not just a case of 'keeping things tidy', but of considering the needs of each child. If you have students who experience particular problems with organisation, then modifying the classroom in small ways can support and help them.

How to help – encouraging self-organisation

☞ **Stationery station.** Set up a station accessible to everyone that has all the resources commonly asked for by students, so that they can use them when needed. This could include glue sticks, a stapler, scissors, tissues, paper towels and so on.

☞ **Help yourself.** Create boxes of helpful resources appropriate to the current tasks for each group or table to share. A numeracy box might include number lines, calculators, rulers, protractors and shape templates. A literacy box might contain key word lists, dictionaries, line guides, story templates or planning sheets.

☞ **What do I do next?** Summarise all the stages of a given task on an overhead transparency or notice board for children to reference in the lesson as a reminder.

☞ **Display a visual timetable.** This could be pinned on a notice board or hung from a washing line, but it should be accessible and visible to everyone in the class.

☞ **Post it!** Ask the children to create bulletin boards with reminders, timetables, and the times of school clubs or team practices. With their creative input a useful asset can become a thing of beauty!

☞ **A magnetic idea.** If you have a magnetic dry wipe board, stick magnetic tape to a container such as a plastic cup and fill it with dry wipe pens, red, blue and black biros and pencils (invaluable for marking the register or marking books).

☞ **Storage solutions.** Make use of hanging storage stations, stick-up cups, transparent pockets and tote bags with lots of useful compartments. Attractive storage solutions encourage both children and adults to use them and be more organised.

☞ **Be prepared!** Before the children come in, collect all the equipment you will need to distribute that day and put it ready in a designated area of the classroom. Be sure to return unused things to storage at the end of the day.

☞ **Label it.** Clearly label storage areas for resources such as painting equipment, maths kit, books and stationery, and ensure that all students are familiar with them. If need be, use pictorial symbols as well as words so that they are accessible to all the children.

☞ **Force of habit.** Establish routines regarding where children should keep their belongings. Labelled drawers, pegs and designated storage areas all help, as well as the expectation that items are returned to their 'home' at the end of a session or the school day.

☞ **Jobs, jobs, jobs.** Try to develop an ethos of joint responsibility for the classroom environment. Children could be given roles that are changed half-termly, such as Librarian (ensures that all the books are stored correctly and recommends books in the class library) or Stationery Officer (ensures all the pencil pots are stocked, collects stray pencils and paper and puts them away).

☞ **Don't erase!** Leave notes on the board as long as possible for children who may require longer to copy them down.

☞ **Make it clear.** Ensure that your presentations on the blackboard or whiteboard are clear and tidy. You could use several different colours for different sections to help students copy accurately.

☞ **Useful words.** Provide a list of key vocabulary for your subject, and display it prominently or provide the list as a handout.

Part 3: Supporting behaviour for learning

Chapter 11: Promoting positive behaviour

For students with attention difficulties, challenging behaviours can often be the first and primary recognition of a need. Children with ADHD struggle with control of impulsive behaviours, distractibility, physical movement and strong emotional reactions, so we need to consider how well our expectations of 'good classroom behaviour' fit with this. As we have noted, it is important not to focus on the diagnosis of ADHD, instead looking to address those behaviours that are proving a real-world challenge and that cause disruption and barriers to learning for the pupils in a classroom.

Key Point

For students with attention difficulties, challenging behaviours can often be the first and primary recognition of a need.

It has been said that all behaviour is a form of communication. If we take this thinking further, all challenging behaviour can be seen as communication of an unmet need. In light of this, it is important to ensure that all necessary support and provision is in place at a universal and targeted level within classrooms, with the Mainstream Core Standards for children and young people with Special Educational Needs and/or disabilities attenting mainstream schools securely in place.[29]

The first challenge in supporting a child with ADHD to manage positive behaviour choices is to get them to 'buy in' to the need to engage with a set of clear, consistent class rules and expectations that the child may feel do not apply to them. A child with low self-esteem, one who is disaffected and disengaged, may lack the sense of belonging and security required to then feel that this set of rules for a class community also apply to them.

Raising self-esteem, and thereby enabling such 'buy in' to rules, can be achieved by promoting positive and secure relationships in the classroom. It has been estimated that children with ADHD often hear 20,000 more negative messages by the time they leave primary education than their neurotypical peers.[30] Coupled with a repeated inability to meet the expectations of teachers and parents, this can cause shame and reluctance

29 Kelsi Inclusion Support Service Kent. https://www.kelsi.org.uk/special-education-needs/special-educational-needs/the-mainstream-core-standards

30 Dodson, W. (2021) *ADHD and the Epidemic of Shame*. Attitude magazine. Url: https://www.additudemag.com/slideshows/adhd-and-shame/

to engage. As we saw in Chapter 7, it is vital that teachers have a clear understanding of the diverse needs within the class, as a children with neurodiverse conditions that result in attention difficulties may well require higher levels of sympathetic supervision than their neurotypical peers.

H2h How to help – promoting positive classroom behaviour

☞ **Phrase rules and messages positively.** Clarity as to what you do rather than don't want conveys positive messages. For example, "Don't shout" could be rephrased as "Use your indoor voice", and "Keep off the grass" could become "Stay on the path."

☞ **Consistency and fairness.** Keep rules consistent from one day to the next, and ensure that this is understood by all children.

☞ **Keep your head when all around are losing theirs.** An unregulated child needs a regulated adult to calm them and make them feel secure. This can be a challenge, and requires a level of self-management.

☞ **Recognise good choices.** Catch children doing the 'right thing' and immediately recognise it; it can be more productive in the long term to tactically ignore some low level negative behaviours.

☞ **Work together to solve challenges.** For example, if a child is struggling to line up for assembly without peer conflict, work together to create a plan to move this forward collaboratively. In addition, asking a pupil where they feel they will focus best and the ideal options for classroom seating for them may well result in the same seating plan that you had hoped for, with the child feeling empowered by that decision.

☞ **Offer choices.** Allowing a child to make decisions – for example which method to use to solve a maths problem, or whether to look online or in a library for research – can raise involvement in their own education.

☞ **Keep it discreet.** Establish a nonverbal warning system between you and the child. This could be a Post-it note on the desk, or even just a hand gesture. Either way it can serve to let the child know that they need to make a change to their current behaviour choices without singling them out in front of their peers.

Strategies to prevent behaviour challenges

Where possible, it is far better to prevent challenging behaviour from happening than to deal with it! In the remainder of this chapter, we will expand on the 'How to Help' advice above to look at pointers for preventing challenging behaviour, and thereby circumventing the need to respond to it.

Supervision levels

Children with ADHD are known to be two to three years behind their neurotypical peers for emotional and social development milestones. This is a vital point when considering your expectations of children with ADHD, as well as when planning your supervision level – for instance during an indoor playtime, or on a school trip. As an illustration, a year three child with ADHD will need the same supervision levels that you would give to a reception aged child during a period of indoor playtime on a wet and windy day!

Routine

Maintaining clear routines provides children with ADHD with a feeling of safety and security in an otherwise stressful world! A routine provides a framework for the children to follow and rely upon, in an environment where children with ADHD and the challenges they face with working memory and attention might find difficult to manage independently. In light of this, wherever possible have clear a routine and structure to your day and week and communicate these with your pupils, preferable visually. Using a visual timetable can be at a class level or, if appropriate, at an individual child level. This can then be adapted when a change of routine is required. Routine and structure will also provide an measure of external control to the pupils in the class with ADHD, for whom self-control can be a challenge.

Choices

Offering forced or fixed choices can be a powerful behaviour management strategy. Offering two choices, rather than simply directing a child to do something, supports children to be involved in their own behaviour management. This can be empowering – who likes being told what to do the whole time? Allowing a child to choose the seat they learn in for that lesson, or who their partner will be, can help them to gain a sense of control as they learn to manage themselves. It can also lead to them doing exactly what you want, as both choices can lead to the same outcome! Offering two choices, both of which you are happy to be taken, can support a child with ADHD as it helps them to manage their time better, relieves the burden on their processing and decision making and provides a safe structure. For example:

- "Eddie, will you fiddle with the cube or the tangle today?"

or

- "James, will you put your Pokémon cards away, or put them on my desk?"

Move, move, move

Children with ADHD are renowned for their need to move – to fidget, wriggle, squirm, toe tap, chair rock and more. Yet ADHD is also associated with periods of stillness, leading some exasperated teachers to say: "They can sit still when they want to!"

Research has shown that this need for movement is heightened when children are accessing the brain's executive functions – which means that it is highlighted at time of cognitive pressure and overload.[31] Allowing built-in movement breaks can avoid the conflict that may occur when a child seeks to meet his or her need for movement within the classroom environment.

---

31 Schlueb, M. (2017) *ADHD Kids Can Be Still – If They're Not Straining Their Brains*. UCF Today.

How to help – managing movement

☞ Provide a whiteboard checklist on the other side of the classroom from where the child with ADHD sits, and allow the child to move and tick off each part of a task when it is completed.

☞ Chop up a maths worksheet into chunks, with each part having to be collected individually from the back of the classroom as the child moves through the questions.

☞ Use pupils with ADHD as message carriers, book distributors and pen collectors. If you need someone to move, choose wisely!

☞ Allow standing work stations, or a designated area of the classroom in which it is agreed that the pupil with ADHD may move around.

☞ Avoid restricting movement as a punishment – for example, making a child with ADHD stay in at playtime to complete unfinished work. Physical activity boosts hormones such as dopamine and serotonin in the brain, both of which support focussed attention. So let them play!

Avoid trigger points

A simple yet productive measure for preventative behaviour management can be to avoid 'trigger moments' – the times when you know that pupils will find managing their behaviour a challenge. A good way to identify these is to traffic light a daily or weekly timetable – this can identify behaviour patterns, stressor lessons and key points in the day that lead to challenges.

Our experience suggests that the points you identify will be times with a lack of structure (lining up for lunch, collecting sports kit from the cloakroom, indoor playtime), times of transition (moving from lesson to lesson, room to room, lunch to register), times where physical needs are not being met (hunger, tiredness, times following lengthy periods of being still) and times of competitiveness (group activities, team sports).

Once the trigger points are identified, small adaptations and adjustments can be made to prevent the situations reoccurring.

How to help – avoiding trigger points

☞ **When hunger strikes.** Changing the lunch sitting to an earlier slot, or having a snack box to access during mid-morning or mid-afternoon can prevent hunger affecting behaviour.

☞ **Lining up a challenge.** Don't line up! Have the student who struggles head into the classroom first and give out the books, or come in via a different door, or be the one who collects the register from the office.

☞ **Cloakroom kerfuffles?** Send children in adequately supervised, and a group at a time. Keep some children back to prep the sports equipment, and then they can change whilst you discuss the activities to the still and ready children. Or – don't use the cloakroom and have a box of sports equipment stored in the classroom!

☞ **Too much sitting still?** Build in whole class movement breaks – some mindfulness, Brain Gym or sensory feedback breaks can be beneficial to the whole class. Also, remember the strategies above for 'Move, move, move' and incorporate a sense of responsibility. Have you appointed the children who crave movement as your book monitors?

☞ **Competition a challenge?** Have set teams to avoid the stressor of team selection, and ensure that rules are clear, concise and followed by all. Smaller teams or groups can be easier for children to manage than larger teams, as there are fewer people to understand and process.

☞ **Indoor playtime.** Ensure that children who will find this a challenge are supervised in a manner that is adequate and appropriate to their stage of social and emotional development, and use all the space available. Having a dedicated space and adult for card games, or using children as buddies in younger classrooms, can help you avoid playtime disasters.

Praise and thanks

Giving a child a direct instruction and ending it with "thank you" conveys the message that this is non-negotiable, that compliance is presumed and that the child has already been thanked for following the instruction successfully!

It is also important that all desirable behaviour is praised. Remembering the poor balance of negative versus positive messages that children with ADHD hear in their childhood, it is vital that they hear positive messages. We will explore the value and role of praise further in the next chapter.

Chapter 12: Responding to behaviour challenges

Despite every conceivable preventative measure being in place, and every possible trigger point having been identified, managed and planned for, there will always be times when behaviour becomes a challenge and conflict or poor behaviour arises. It is important to develop strategies and response measures to deal with these situations in a forward-looking way. And this is not easy – developing effective behaviour strategies, working preventatively and addressing issues positively can be time consuming, exhausting and relentless. But when we put the effort in, we reap the rewards!

Key Point

Despite every preventative measure being in place, there will always be times when behaviour becomes a challenge and conflict arises.

There are two key pointers when managing positive behaviour in a responsive manner for children with ADHD. Firstly, we need to reinforce desired behaviours using praise and rewards. And secondly, we need to be decreasing the problem behaviours, with clear limits and consequences.

It is vitally important, as already mentioned, that we praise more than we criticise. For pupils with ADHD, who are constantly living in the moment, making impulsive decisions and reacting rather than responding, this is even more paramount. Look for the behaviour that you desire, catch it happening in the moment, and praise it immediately! Real time recognition is key: wait too long and the desired behaviour may pass, leaving you to note only negative behaviour with the opportunity for praise and recognition lost.

The desired behaviour can be one key thing that you have all agreed to work on – for example, raising a hand to answer a question rather than shouting out. As soon as you see this happen, even if you are not asking that particular child for the answer at that moment, recognise it. Recognition could take the form of a bookmark on the table which earns a tick, a jar kept on the windowsill where a marble or button is placed, or even a simple thumbs up. As long as the child knows that the praise is for them, and understands exactly how it was earned, then it is working to support them in identifying the positive behaviours that you are looking for. These collective recognitions of positive behaviour choices can also work towards earning rewards, which again should be agreed upon in advance.

In a more general sense, 'catching' a child making a good behaviour choice in the moment is an ongoing positive reinforcement for the child. Be it attending to a task without adult support, sharing resources readily with a peer, or collecting materials independently, catching the child in the act and specifically praising the desired behaviour is paramount. The praise can be verbal – "Emma, I love that you're sharing the glue so readily with Jess" or it can take other forms. Small 'Catch Me Cards' with good behaviour choices noted and posted into a 'golden box' for collation, sharing and praise at the end of the day are a great way to make this recognition visual and tangible.

All humans crave human attention. By providing positive affirmation through specific praise for desired behaviour, we provide that much-needed attention, and teach children that this is how to get it. This goes hand in hand with some tactical ignoring of low level disruptive behaviours that may also be happening. Reacting to these behaviours, even in a negative way, still provides feedback and attention for the child. It takes a shift of focus and approach to look for the good and ignore the not-so-good, but by doing so a powerful uplift in positivity can result.

It is vitally important that all teachers working with children, neurotypical as well as neurodiverse, do not take away rewards that have already been given. Rewarding a child with ticks, stars or marbles for not calling out of turn and then taking them away when the same child shouts or interferes with a peer's resources gives a negative message – that it is not worth trying to earn rewards as they can be easily withdrawn. The consequence of the negative behaviour should be to get no reward for that behaviour – not to lose rewards gained for previous good behaviour.

When things do go wrong, as they will, deal with the situation fairly, calmly and productively. Talk to the child about what has happened: sit eye to eye, speak calmly and listen not to respond but to understand. Whenever speaking to a child with ADHD in a busy classroom, always start with their name to gain their attention, pause briefly to ensure that they have processed that you are speaking to them, and then continue!

A powerful strategy for supporting the talking it through process for children who may have impaired perceptions of memories of events, can be to use Comic Strip Conversations. This is a visual technique developed by Carol Gray.[32] It was initially produced to support children with autism to develop greater social understanding, but has also been used successfully to support children with ADHD to understand the various parts that individuals played in an incident gone wrong. The Comic Strip Conversation uses stick figures to give visual representations of the communication that happened between people, both verbal and non verbal, and it can be a useful tool in helping to recall a sequence of events from one's own and others' perceptions before trying to restore relationships and move on.

Restorative justice

Restorative Justice techniques were initially created as an approach within the criminal justice system, bringing the perpetrators and victims of crime together to find positive ways forward through shared understanding and dialogue. However, they are increasingly being embraced by schools and youth movements as a means to structure and support purposeful, restorative conversations with children following social falling out.

The children's services organisation Salus Group (www.salusgroup.org.uk) uses and recommends the following questioning profile:

1. What's happened?
2. What were you thinking?
3. How were you feeling?
4. Who has been affected or upset?
5. What do you need to make things better?
6. How can we move forward?

This questioning profile, supported with visual aids (such as Comic Strip Conversations) takes place with everyone involved – be it a group of children who have fallen out in the playground, or a pupil and a teacher who have come into conflict. It should take place in a circle (non-confrontational) with each member of the group having a fair amount of time to talk and be heard. The use of a talking object (such as a pebble or a soft toy) to indicate who is talking can help to organise everyone. The approach is built on the principles of restorative justice, with the aim of avoiding the same things happening again, and 'fixing' what has failed rather than being punitive.

---

32 Gray, C. (1994). *Comic Strip Conversations: Illustrated Interactions that Teach Conversation Skills to Students with Autism and Related Disorders*. Jenison, MI.: Jenison Public Schools.

For children with ADHD, it can often seem as if they do not learn from their mistakes, and that consequences do not have the desired impact of changing the behaviour. This is partly because these young people, who live in the moment and react to events and emotions within that moment, are not able to pause, to think, and to make working memory links to previous experiences. All these actions are required in order for children to make a connection between behaviour and consequence, and this is the first step in the process of them making an informed decision about what to do next!

How to help – sanctions and consequences

☞ Every school will operate its own Behaviour policy, with its own rewards and sanctions built in. If your school operates a sanction and consequence approach, then it is important when dealing with children with ADHD that the consequences are logical, reasonable, fair, timed and consistent. Bear in mind that taking a playtime away from a child with ADHD can have a negative outcome for all involved by removing a much needed movement break in the day.

☞ Ensure that any consequence given to a child with ADHD is reflective of their developmental age and be clear, before the event if possible, what the consequence will be by using an "If-Then" approach:

■ "Daniel, IF you throw the maths resources on the floor again, THEN you will have to work alone outside the classroom."

■ "Jenna, IF you choose to doodle on your maths book not your pad, THEN you will have to rewrite your maths problems."

☞ Obviously, before either of these eventualities are reached they should have been dealt with using a fixed choice approach to avoid the confrontation and negative choice:

■ "Daniel, would you find it easier to use the maths resources at your work station OR in a tray?"

■ "Jenna, I can see that you need to doodle, will you use your pad OR some scrap paper?"

Chapter 13: Why don't they listen?

One might easily believe that listening is a passive activity, but it's actually an active process. We have to make a conscious effort to hear what someone's saying, and by doing so we make that person feel understood. Good listening shows others that they're important to us, so naturally when our listening skills improve, so do our relationships.

Key Point

Good listening shows others that they're important to us, so naturally when our listening skills improve, so do our relationships.

It is often said that there are two main types of listening. The first is listening in order to reply. The second is listening in order to understand, otherwise known as active listening. It is actually a myth that the greatest salespeople are the fastest talkers; in reality it is the active listeners who are best able to understand and deliver exactly what the customer wants.

While effective listening is a highly regarded social skill, it doesn't come easily to people with ADHD who have a hard time concentrating and are easily distracted. Most individuals with ADHD are impulsive talkers – they have listening difficulties and they listen to reply. Individuals with inattentive type ADHD may not be great talkers, but as they often have hypoactivity they may be mental drifters – again with a low level of active listening skills.

How to help – improving active listening skills

☞ Here are some tips to improve active listening skills among children with impulsive/hyperactive type ADHD:

- Slow down. A breath between sentences will help you control the rush of words bursting out of your mouth and give others a chance to take in what you have to say.

- Wait your turn. ADHD 'talkers' have difficulty controlling the impulse to jump in and interrupt. Aside from being annoying to others, this behavior makes it hard to focus on what someone is saying. When someone is speaking, concentrate on waiting until they end their sentence before jumping in. If you have a question, ask permission before asking: "Excuse me, may I ask a question?"

■ Talk about what you hear. When someone is talking to you, focus on finding a key point to comment on, rather than running off in all directions. This lets others know that you're listening, helps you to follow along, and opens the door to social acceptance.

■ See what you hear. To think about what someone is saying to you, visualise the story in your mind. Pretend that you'll be quizzed, and that you'll have to describe the conversation. Could you do it?

 Here are some tips to improve active listening skills among children with inattentive/distractible type ADHD:

■ Compete for their focus. Try to work out the main distractors (auditory, visual, kinaesthetic, internal) in the classroom environment, and look at ways in which these can be managed.

■ Hold their interest. Make sure that tasks are as interesting as possible to minimise susceptibility to distractions, and match tasks to ability so that the children are challenged but not dispirited.

■ Keep them busy. Provide something to 'fiddle' with, particularly in seated situations with lengthy periods of listening; keeping the hands occupied can help a child with ADHD to listen and focus.

■ Keep track of time. Understanding time and time limits is difficult for children with ADHD. Egg timers are useful to indicate how long is left in a task, and as a means to track length of conversation.

Can't or won't?

The majority of children with ADHD, as we have seen, have very real problems with listening. However, what about those who can listen but simply choose not to, and actually push back at all attempts to help them engage with learning? There are two terms given to describe persistent oppositional behaviour. The first term is 'Oppositional Defiant Disorder' (ODD) and the second is 'Pathological Demand Avoidance' (PDA).

Children with Oppositional Defiant Disorder tend to exhibit the following persistent behaviours (beyond those normally expected of their age group):

- Angry and irritable
- Often lose their temper
- Argue with authority and refuse to comply with requests or rules
- Often deliberately annoy people and blame others for mistakes
- Spiteful or vindictive
- Often argue with adults
- Often actively defy or refuse to comply with adult requests or rules
- Often appear touchy or easily annoyed by others
- Often appear angry or resentful

Pathological Demand Avoidance is an anxiety-driven need to be in control, characterised by extreme avoidance of everyday demands. Key features are:

- Refusing to comply with requests
- Giving excuses
- Distracting or changing the subject
- Negotiating or needing to have the last word
- Bombarding with repetitive questions or noises
- Withdrawing into fantasy worlds
- Complaining of physical impairment – 'my legs won't work'
- Panic-driven physical outbursts or meltdowns

Children with PDA share many of the communication, social interaction and sensory difficulties that characterise the autism spectrum, and as a result PDA and autism often occur together. The causes of ODD are not well understood but it is thought that a combination of environmental and biological factors may be involved including parenting issues, abuse or neglect, traumatic experiences such as a marriage break-up, family mental health issues, underachievement and natural disposition or temperament.

H2h How to Help How to help – managing oppositional behaviour

Children with ODD and PDA are often demanding, difficult and defiant, so management both at school and at home takes time, energy, hard work and commitment. There are no magic solutions to transform behaviours overnight. The key is to establish consistent approaches at school and at home, and to work in close collaboration. The tips below are a starting point only, as specific children will require specific systems and strategies.

☞ Tips for teachers and schools:

- Identify what triggers the child's behaviour
- Develop classroom rules and a daily schedule
- Provide structure during free time or break times
- Communicate clearly both rewards and consequences
- Be positive: give praise and positive reinforcement
- Do not provide opportunities to argue
- Avoid raising your voice: be neutral and speak calmly
- Put the child near a good role model
- Minimise distractions

☞ Tips for parents and carers:

- Create a structured environment: set house rules, routines and expectations
- Be clear and consistent
- Use a calm voice
- Pick your battles and avoid power struggles
- Learn to play with your child, and spend time together
- Celebrate successes and praise good behaviour
- Assign a weekly household chore
- Persevere: behaviour is likely to get worse before it gets better

Chapter 14: Self-regulation

The skill of self-regulation goes by many names including self-control, impulse control, anger management and emotional regulation. In a nutshell, these all mean the same thing. They describe firstly a person's alertness to their current emotional state, and secondly their ability to choose how to portray that emotional state through their behaviour.

Key Point

Self-regulation is a person's alertness to their emotional state, and their ability to choose how to portray that state through their behaviour.

All children lose control, and all children have emotional meltdowns – be it due to anger, hurt, sadness, frustration or annoyance. But for children with ADHD, this is even more of a difficulty. Issues with managing impulsivity due to the neurological nature of their disorder mean that they lack the control to consider the consequences of lashing out in anger, to stop themselves from bursting into tears with frustration, or to think better of shouting at a teacher when they feel that something is unfair. This lack of 'pause and think', or putting the brakes on, can limit the self-regulation or control that neurodiverse children possess in comparison to their neurotypical peers.

Several other factors can make self-regulation more difficult for a child with ADHD. As they are developmentally up to three years behind their neurotypical peers they may lack the language and vocabulary needed to express themselves adequately in times of emotional turmoil. They will struggle to learn from their mistakes, as we saw in Chapter 8, as a result of their lack of working memory coupled with the impulsive nature of their behaviour. Their mood and emotional regulation may be affected by comorbid conditions such as anxiety, depression or oppositional defiant disorder. And of course, many children with ADHD take medication – which can wear off prior to the next dose, causing the child to be more irritable and upset and allowing their emotions to bubble up out of control.

Why do we need to develop self-regulation?

Self-regulation enables a child to make behavioural choices that allow them to be in the best possible emotional state at a given moment in time. It is prerequisitie for students to form secure and successful relationships with their peers, to access learning, to raise self-esteem and create a positive mindset, and to to generate a positive sense of self and belonging. Children who 'lose control' can be perceived by their peers as unpredictable, and therefore unsafe friends. This will obviously have a negative impact on potential friendships, and subsequently on self-esteem and sense of community, all of which are vital to successful lifelong learning.

Leah Kuypers, the developer of the 'Zones of Regulation' concept, argues that self-regulation "includes regulating one's sensory needs, emotion and impulses to meet the demands of the environment, reach one's goals and behave in a socially appropriate way."[33] Quite a challenge for a child who may already face numerous situations each day where they feel frustrated, overwhelmed, overstimulated, misunderstood, tired, confused or upset!

Kuypers goes on to discuss three 'critical neurological components' required to successfully self-regulate:

1. Sensory Processing: making sense of the input from our senses
2. Executive Functioning: attention, processing and memory
3. Emotional Regulation: understanding and responding to our emotions

As all of the above are areas of difficulty for children with ADHD, and as all three are required for successful self-regulation, it is apparent that self-regulation is an area where our students with attention difficulties will require significant support and help.

Mastering self-regulation

In order for them to develop skills of self-control and learn to regulate their own emotions successfully, children must go through a number of stages. The process could be structured and described as follows:

Stage 1: Naming emotions

For children to work on managing their emotions, they first need to be able to describe them! Photo card images, emojis, Lego figures or storybooks can be excellent starting points for naming a range of emotions. It is important to also explore alternative words for the same emotions – don't just stick with happy or sad! Creating word banks linked to images is a vital starting point for successful work on self-regulation. Games such as emotions bingo, with visual images and keywords attached, can help to reinforce vocabulary.

---

33 Kuypers, L. (2011). *The Zones of Regulation: A Curriculum Designed to Foster Self-Regulation and Emotional Control.* Santa Clara, CA.: Think Social Publishing.

Stage 2: Categorising emotions

The named emotions next need to be categorised as 'comfortable' or 'uncomfortable'. This can be done powerfully through colour, and can be an interesting group exercise to compare and contrast how different emotions are tolerated by different people. For example, for one person surprise may be an exciting and positive feeling; but for another, the unknown can cause great discomfort. An interesting conversation starter!

Stage 3: Reading emotions

Once emotions have been named and sorted, the next stage is to work on reading them, in other words understanding how they make us feel and behave. When children are in the early stages of learning to self-regulate, naming what we are able to see by observing them is a powerful first step.

- "Emma, I can see that you're feeling angry at the moment as you've clenched your fists"
- "David, I can see that you're feeling frustrated because your head is in your hands and you're breathing quickly."

When children are 'out of control', they are at the mercy of their primal brain. Also known as the 'reptilian brain', this controls instinctual thinking and behaviour, and 'hardwires' us to react instantly to danger, whether real or imagined. A tiny structure called the amygdala orders the release of stress hormones which direct oxygen to our limbs, so that we are ready to respond via Fight, Flight, Freeze or Flock. However, this leaves insufficient fuel to power other parts of the brain fully. So our more evolved brain – the neocortex human brain, built to make make informed judgements and decisions but operating at a slower rate – is hijacked by our primal brain!

We have all experienced situations where we were at the peak of our emotional volcano, in full 'caveman mode' – and afterwards, we had little clear recollection of what happened. We can revisit and know that our choices were not made with the best judgement, and we often wish we had said or done something differently. Unfortunately, the heightened level of stress hormone in the brain can also affect the neurons, with an impact on short term memory. So when you ask a child what has happened or why they did something, the response "I don't remember" may well be the truth.

For a child to grasp what is going on at this level may seem a challenge, but the use of some simple tools and brain models can help us understand what is going on inside when we are 'losing it'. Through these methods, we can support children to make links between parts of their brain not working effectively, and the impact that this has on their bodies and behaviour.

'The Red Beast' by K I Al-Ghani is a useful lesson in how emotions can affect our behaviour.[34] This child-friendly picture book teaches children that, at the height of anger, our eyes shrink so we can't see what is going on, our ears shrink so we can't hear what people are saying to us, and our mouths grow so we shout at those around us. This can be a useful starting point to discuss what other physical reactions make be taking place:

Expert View

"Deep inside everyone a Red Beast lies sleeping, When it is asleep the Red Beast is quite small. However, when it wakes up, it begins to grow and grow."

K.I. Al-Ghan

- Do you have heat anywhere in your body? Face? Hands?
- Does your body feel restless? Jittery feet? Can't be still?
- Are your hands clenched into fists?
- Is your face scrunched up? Are your teeth clenched?
- Are you breathing quickly?

These conversations can take place as part of a group – mixing neurodiverse and neurotypical children. This gives a strong message to the neurodiverse children that everyone feels anger; some of us just have sleepier red beasts!

Once their physical and physiological responses have been identified, the children need to identify what behaviour they are currently using to portray their emotion. For example, are they displaying a feeling of anger by kicking their peers? Are they displaying frustration by shouting and swearing? Splitting the emotion and the behaviour into separate categories helps children identify what they can do to start taking control.

Stage 4: Identifying triggers for emotions

Once work has taken place on naming, categorising and reading emotions, the next stage to work on is supporting children to identify what causes them to feel these emotions. Again, this may need to be a stage where, as observing adults, we kick things off by naming the emotions and behaviour that we can see – remembering to wait for the children to be calm!

---

34 Al-Ghani, K.I. (2008) *The Red Beast: Controlling Anger in Children with Asperger's Syndrome.* London: Jessica Kingsley.

Use event or situation cards as conversation starters – how would you react to this event? How would this situation make you feel? Using real-life situations makes learning relevant and purposeful with starters such as:

- You can't find your homework that you worked really hard on.
- Someone pushes in-front of you in the lunch line.
- You are playing tag and you are caught on 'it'.
- You have your hand up in class and nobody picks you.
- The classroom is noisy and nobody is listening to you.
- Football club is cancelled because it's too rainy and wet.
- Someone has taken your pen from your desk without asking.
- Your friend interrupts you when you are speaking.

Also try to use scenarios generated by the children, and examples from outside school. Create a bank of situations and use these to explore:

1. Naming feelings – what emotion would this trigger?
2. Sensations - what would happen to my body?
3. Actions - what behaviour would I show?

Again, undertaking this activity in groups can support diversity as well as acceptance, and also enable less emotionally literate children to learn vocabulary, language and skills from their peers.

Stage 5: Scaling emotions

Due to the rapid and immediate nature of experiencing intense emotions, and the reactive and impulsive responses that children with ADHD then tend to feel, learning to 'put the brakes on' can often be a challenge. When working with children who find this difficult, using scaling techniques to add measurable values and comparative features into the mix can support many of them in understanding the need to slow down, calculate and process responses. Scaled numerical systems can also provide real visual aids.

There are many commercially available systems – two of them are 'The Zones of Regulation' by Leah Kuypers[33] and 'The Incredible 5 Point Scale' by Kari Burron.[35] Both are structured but also flexible regarding the needs and ages of children. They can be used successfully with children as young as six, with adaptations if needed to make things simpler. With

35 Burron, K., & Curtis, M. (2012). *The Incredible 5-Point Scale: Assisting Students in Understanding Social Interactions and Controlling Their Emotional Responses.* Shawnee KS.: AAPC Publishing.

older children, they can be used in small groups as well as individually. When an explosive child walks to the cloakroom and says: "I can't go in – it will make me a 5!", you will know that you've had a positive impact on their self-regulation skills.

In addition to its role as a teaching tool in schools, scaling can also be used successfully as a basis for up-skilling families and therefore helping them to manage behaviour at home. This can be a simple yet effective way to support parents and carers, ensuring a common approach and language is used across both settings as well as raising wellbeing of the children when in school.

Chapter 15: Dealing with dysregulation

When a child is dysregulated – when their volcano has exploded and they have 'lost it' – they need a toolkit of effective strategies to calm themselves, return to comfortable emotions and move themselves back down the scale to a regulated state. This toolkit will be different for each individual, with different strategies being useful at varying positions on the scale.

It is important when working with children to involve them fully in the creation of such a toolkit – to discuss which strategies prevent us escalating, and to know when they will be effective. For example, when Emma feels that she is bubbling at a '2', with hot hands and fidgety feet, she may know some hand breathing will help. However, if Emma has hit a '4' or even a '5', and is shouting and lashing out, then she may know that hand breathing will not be effective. Talking through each stage and discussing triggers, body cues and real-life incidents with mind mapping of ideas is the only way to effectively plan individual de-escalation strategies.

Once strategies have been created and written with the child, it is vital for success to share this with all adults working with the child. Consistent messages and approaches allow this to be a trustworthy strategy that a child can rely on and have faith in, providing a sense of security and safety.

How to help – calming techniques

☞ Preventiative strategies:

- **Self-care.** Ensure that self-care is in place. Are you fed? Are you rested? Are you warm?
- **Mindfulness.** Mindfulness can be used to support the calming process.
- **Yoga.** Yoga helps develop awareness of body and mind.
- **Exercise.** Exercise releases endorphins ('happy hormones') and aids restful sleep.

☞ Reactive strategies:

- **Popping bubble wrap.** This is systematic, distracting and calming
- **Blowing bubbles.** This encourages deep breathing, allowing oxygen to reach the thinking brain!
- **Deep breathing.** This increases the supply of oxygen to the brain and subsequently stimulates the parasympathetic nervous system, which promotes a state of calmness. This can be done using visual cues, for example hand breaths. Lay one hand on your lap or the desk, and use the other to trace around your hand, Breathe in on a finger up, and out on a finger down.
- **Music.** Use of a headset can help to block out and escape from triggers, as well as diverting the brain and focus from challenges.
- **Safe den.** Somewhere to hide and get away to use as an escape can offer a calming sanctuary. Children often like this to be a covered space – perhaps a tepee, under a table, or in a den.
- **Energy release.** Provide an outlet to release pent up physical energy in a healthy way. This may be on a large scale, for example kicking a ball into a goal, bouncing on a trampoline or running. Or it could be on a much smaller scale, for example:
  - scribbling in an 'angry book'
  - screwing up paper strips as small as you can
  - having a box of scrap paper to tear up into tiny pieces

- punching or squeezing a stress toy or playdough
- Punching or shouting into a pillow or cushion

Whichever outlet you choose, try to dispose of the negative energy. Shake the cushion full of angry words out of the window; throw the scribbled and torn paper into the bin. This gives a clear visual cue that the anger is gone and is no longer part of the child!

Dealing with anger

Anger can be scary. It is an emotion that we try to shy away from, for fear of what it means and how it makes us behave. Yet anger is also a necessary emotion, and one that is designed to preserve, motivate and protect us.

It is important to recognise that anger is a real feeling, and that we all have the right to experience anger when we feel our needs are not being met. This is important because if you don't at least recognise that a person is angry, even if you don't agree with the cause of their anger, then they will become even angrier and eventually this may turn into rage. At this point you will have a major problem on your hands, and there is a risk that your relationship will be seriously undermined and compromised.

One of the simplest yet most important things for a child who has difficulties with self-regulation to learn is this:

All feelings are okay.

This message is vital for a child who is struggling to control their emotional responses. Without it, we can shy away from uncomfortable feelings – be they anger, fear or irritation. Such feelings are within us, but we need not be categorised or labelled by them. A simple language adjustment to support children who struggle with anger can be to move from:

"Why are you so angry, John?"

to

"What is causing you to feel anger, John?"

This subtle shift dehumanises the emotion and makes it something that the child can deal with. The anger doesn't define them; it's a feeling that they are experiencing, and they just need a more healthy response to manage it.

Key messages to share with everybody are therefore:

- Anger is an emotion
- Emotions are healthy
- We need a safe and healthy behaviour to express our anger

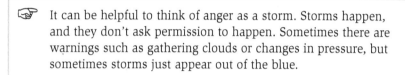

How to help – the anger storm

☞ It can be helpful to think of anger as a storm. Storms happen, and they don't ask permission to happen. Sometimes there are warnings such as gathering clouds or changes in pressure, but sometimes storms just appear out of the blue.

☞ The key is always to monitor mood. Key warning signs for an approaching anger storm are:

- The voice getting louder
- Mutterings under the teeth
- Repetitive body movements such as tapping and rocking
- Screwing up paper or scribbling on a page
- Changes in eye contact

☞ If you notice warnings of an anger storm, you need to deploy mood management techniques quickly to defuse the situation:

- Get in quickly and be positive
- Divert the child's attention to something else
- Relocate the child within the classroom
- Make a change in your teaching style
- Adopt calming body language
- Use humour

☞ Once the storm passes, it is critical to rebuild the relationship by listening to the angry person and accepting their version of events. Don't judge the person, and make it clear that you are seriously considering the information that you have been given – even if it is inconsistent with what you yourself feel took place.

Chapter 16: Developing rapport, relationships and resilience

There was a time when people in education referred to the '3Rs', meaning "reading, 'riting and 'rithmetic". Coined around the start of the 19th century, this expression prioritised reading, writing and arithmetic as the three key pillars on which to build the basics of an educational system. Today, in terms of supporting the challenges faced by children and young people with ADHD, the three pillars of education might well be reclassified as "rapport, relationships and resilience." It is vital to secure the trust and goodwill of young people who have struggled with attention difficulties, and supporting this requires the building of firm bonds with both adults and peers along the way. Finally, there will come a time when individuals must self-regulate and deal by themselves with the stressors associated with the choices they make. Building the rapport, relationships and resilience will provide the foundations for this journey of development to take place.

Key Point

In terms of supporting young people with ADHD, the three pillars of education might be reclassified as "rapport, relationships and resilience."

Rapport

The word 'rapport' derives from the French verb *rapporter*, meaning 'to bring back'. And 'bringing back' is exactly what we must do with some of our students with challenging behaviour – we need to bring them back from the brink of negative choices that they may be about to make.

In modern English, 'rapport' is a noun meaning 'a close and harmonious relationship in which the people or groups concerned understand each other's feelings or ideas and communicate well.' Now, communication is of course something that we all do every day. But what can we do to improve or fine-tune it?

Albert Mehrabian, a California psychology professor, was one of the first advocates for the power of nonverbal communication.[36] His extensive research on the topic of body language resulted in the '7-38-55 rule', which states that communication is:

- 7% words
- 38% tonality, volume and tempo
- 55% nonverbal signals

Expert View

"Our speech-oriented culture is just beginning to take note of the profound and overlooked contribution of nonverbal behaviour to communication."

Albert Mehrabian

Mehrabian's central point is that most of what we communicate is not about the words we choose – it's about how they're delivered. Messages only have their maximum impact when you can see how words are transmitted by a person. As an example, think about text messages on a phone. We can see the words, but we have no idea of the feelings behind them. When we speak to someone by phone we get a better understanding; but the full power of a message is only conveyed when we can see the person actually saying the words.

Generating rapport is not always easy, but it is a vital step towards structure and flexibility. Once rapport is established, you can then move on to the next level of interpersonal communication which is building positive relationships.

---

36 Mehrabian, A. (1981). *Silent messages: Implicit communication of emotions and attitudes (2d ed.)*. Belmont, CA.: Wadsworth Publishing.

How to help – generating rapport

When working with and supporting children and young people with challenging behaviours, there are steps that we can take in order to maximise the impact and value of our communication.

☞ Make the most of nonverbal signals and body language:

- ■ Eye contact – be flexible at all times
- ■ Height and positioning – level with the individual
- ■ Appear relaxed, and do not make fidgeting movements
- ■ Use facial expressions and lots of nodding
- ■ Balance closeness with personal space
- ■ Employ focused and active listening

☞ Key tips for active listening:

- ■ Give your complete focus to what the other person is saying
- ■ Let the other person finish before you start talking
- ■ Maintain eye contact wherever possible
- ■ Keep your emotions in check
- ■ Do not interrupt or jump to conclusions
- ■ Look for the feelings or intent behind the words

☞ Useful phrases for starting conversations with reluctant learners:

- ■ "Let's…"
- ■ "I need you to…"
- ■ "In five minutes you will have…"
- ■ "Today we're going to…"
- ■ "I know that you will…"
- ■ "Thank you for…"

Relationships

Human beings are driven to form relationships with other people. Indeed, the survival and evolution of our species depends on this. Schools are places where deep and meaningful relationships occur within a community that is unique to itself, but also similar to other schools in terms of the nature and relative importance of those relationships. The three main sets of relationships that occur are as shown below:

Key Point

Any relationship is a two way process; neither party should take it for granted, and both parties need to work on it.

- Student and teacher
- Peer to peer
- Teacher and teacher (or other member of staff)

The key relationship for this book is of course student to teacher; we have seen how this can take place, and how students prefer their teacher to be a teacher and not a friend. Any relationship is, however, a two way process; neither party should take it for granted, and both parties need to work on it. The teacher will obviously be the key player in the relationship, and will need to observe the key issues of structure and flexibility, but there is also the question of providing feedback on student behaviour choices. This will tend to involve rewards and sanctions in line with the school Behaviour Policy.

Rewards and sanctions - rewards

A reward is given as the result of good behaviour – and more specifically, in this context, in recognition of behaviour choices that are in the child's best interest. Needless to say, every child (and also every adult!) likes rewards – whether they take the form of stickers, house points, freedom of movement, school trips or something else. Yet the most effective reward of all is praise from someone with whom you have a good relationship.

There is a story about a highly respected Premier League football manager who, after training each day, would slip a Polo mint into the bag of the player who had put in the best performance. All the players were multi-millionaires with mansions and supercars, so money mattered very little to them; the talk each day was of who had got the Polo, because that was the person who had been singled out for the manager's praise. The reward had negligible value, yet it was actively sought after for what it represented.

Praise is a vital cog in any teacher-pupil relationship, and its importance cannot be overstated. The giving of praise can to some extent be codified as an objective science; however, one must keep a number of factors in mind:

- Praise should be seen as one component part of an ongoing process of wider encouragement.
- It is important to distinguish between praise given for task completion and personal praise.
- Praise will have different effects according to the gender, home background, abilities and personalities of pupils.
- Praise can improve self-esteem, self-reliance, autonomy, motivation and achievement.

Rewards and sanctions - sanctions

Sanctions are things that children do not like - for instance a detention, or a loss of privilege. Most children won't like being given a sanction but they will usually accept them - albeit reluctantly. While sanctions should not be desirable, they should not be physically or psychologically harmful, and it is important to note that they do not have to be severe to be effective. It is not the severity but the certainty that has an impact. The ultimate sanction is to be told by someone who you know values you, and with whom you have a good relationship, that you have disappointed them.

There may be times when a sanction is not accepted - usually when it is delivered in a way that embarrasses or threatens the child, and causes them to react badly. To avoid such situations, it is important to remember not to:

- Shout at the students
- Ignore their views
- Stand too close or aggressively face-to-face
- Bring up past unrelated misdemeanours
- Raise your voice in an effort to be the loudest
- Be nonverbally aggressive e.g. with arm flailing, facial expressions
- Allow conflict in a public forum

Often these behaviours will generate a 'fight or flight' reaction in the child, and this may be a precursor to anger. Should this happen, you will need to use the techniques described in Chapter 15 to quickly defuse the situation.

Rewards and sanctions – problem solving toolkit

If your rewards and sanctions system is not working, it is important to reflect on why this is the case. A problem-solving checklist should provide you with a picture of the situation that can be used as the basis for adjustment:

- When do the problems occur? (e.g. time of day, specific situations)
- What are the triggers? (e.g. interaction with particular classmates, boredom, specific tasks)
- In confrontational situations how does he or she react?
- In what ways does your own response affect the outcome?
- What seems to have a positive effect? (e.g. your approach, use of humour, change of task)

Resilience

Having developed rapport and relationships, there is one more component required to allow structure and flexibility in our classrooms – and to enable students to be at once independent and dependent on us as adults. We need to take the stabilisers off and begin to develop and facilitate resilience.

Resilience appears to involve several interrelated elements. Firstly, it is to do with a sense of self-esteem and confidence. Secondly, it requires a belief in one's own self-efficacy and ability to deal with change and adaptation. And thirdly, it means having a repertoire of social problem-solving approaches.

- Positive factors for resilience in a child are:
  - Secure early relationships
  - Being female
  - Higher intelligence
  - Easy temperament when an infant
  - Positive attitude, problem-solving approach
  - Good communication skills
  - Planner, belief in control
  - Humour
  - Religious faith

- Positive factors for resilience in a family are:
  - At least one good parent-child relationship
  - Affection
  - Clear, firm and consistent discipline
  - Support for education
  - Supportive long term relationship/absence of severe discord

- Positive factors for resilience in a community are:
  - Wider supportive network
  - Good housing
  - High standard of living
  - A school with positive policies on behaviour, attitudes and anti-bullying
  - Opportunities for valued social roles
  - A range of sport and leisure activities

- Positive factors for resilience in a school are:
  - Clear policies on behaviour and bullying
  - Open door policy for children to raise concerns
  - A whole school approach to promoting good mental health
  - Positive classroom management
  - A sense of belonging
  - Positive peer influence

Part 4: Working in partnership with others

Chapter 17: How can I support the families of children with ADHD?

The SEND Code of Practice[22] is very clear as to the importance of of schools working effectively with parents, and it is widely agreed that meaningful partnerships can generate huge potential benefits. Judy McKnight has argued that parents know their children best and are "their first and most important teachers"[37], and the Lamb Inquiry into special educational needs and parent confidence also noted that parental engagement with their children's education can have a significant positive impact on outcomes.[38]

Despite this weight of evidence, establishing an effective parent relationship can be one of the biggest challenges when supporting pupils with additional needs. An issue faced by education professionals is that while parents are experts on their children's needs, they often face personal difficulties without knowing the best way to support them. ADHD has a higher genetic correlation than some cancers, so in many cases the parents may well be managing their own attention and focus problems, whether diagnosed or not. This adds a futher layer of challenge, with some parents having an apprehension and reluctance to engage with their children's education due to the poor support they experienced during their own school years.

As a result of these issues, parents frequently seek a level of support and advice from the education professionals they come into contact with – often, the only professionals that they have easy access to. With lengthening waiting times to see medical professionals and educational psychologists, it is not surprising that class teachers and SENCOs are the first port of call for parents who need help and guidance in supporting

---

37 McKnight, J. (1989). Parents are 'Experts' on Their Children. EducationWeek opinion piece, November 29th 1989.

38 Lamb, B. (2009). Lamb Inquiry Special Educational Needs and Parental Confidence. Annesley: DCSF Publications.

their children. And in view of this, it is paramount that the relationship is one of equals, where both voices feel heard and work together for the benefit of the child.

Time to talk

Parenting a child with ADHD can be a hugely rewarding experience, but it can also bring a multitude of challenges. Trying to get the support a child needs can be frustrating, exhausting and scary. The relentless conveyor belt of adaptations that may be needed to support a child, and the daily battles that can occur – particularly with transitions from home to school – can lead to feelings of loneliness and isolation, with parents often not sharing their worries with others for fear of being judged or a lack of understanding. Many feel scared for their child's future, and expect the next stage of their son or daughter's childhood to bring yet another mountain to climb.

In the light of these difficulties, it is vital that education professionals are as supportive as possible. The aim should be a relationship where parents feel able to approach a teacher or SENCO for a nod of understanding or a friendly ear – not just for formal solutions. Listen to understand, don't take negativity personally, and remember that you are speaking with another human being who may have spent a long time building up the courage to begin this conversation – so smile and be kind. A parent approaching a teacher for advice is not a SEND review meeting and it should not be treated in the same way. Whether parents are seeking a shoulder to cry on or an emotional punchbag, when they come with their challenges and concerns it is important that the teacher is ready to respond appropriately.

To ensure that a positive and reciprocal talking relationship is established between parents and staff, it is important to be especially sensitive and careful when holding formal SEND meetings. These can be daunting and overwhelming for parents of children with additional needs, and as a result they are not always welcomed with open arms. The SEND Code of Practice has clear required outcomes from initial parent meetings, stating that they should be structured in such a way as to develop a good understanding of the pupil's areas of strength and difficulty, the parents' concerns, the agreed outcomes sought for the child and the next steps. But whether it is the first meeting with the family or the tenth, there are factors for school staff to consider. Some of these are explored below.

How to help – holding effective SEND meetings

☞ **Schedule sensitively.** Always involve parents in agreeing a mutually acceptable time to meet, as starting discussions with a formal letter dictating time and place can set the wrong tone and lead to a parent feeling alienated before you've begun. Try a phone call, a friendly chat at the school gate or a less formal email as a starting point, and ask when they are available to meet so that the parent feels in control.

☞ **Be welcoming to all.** Be prepared with a box of toys or books for little ones, and appropriately sized chairs for everybody attending. Sitting in a circle is less confrontational than sitting face to face, and creates an atmosphere of equality and openness. Perhaps put the kettle on and offer a cup of tea before you kick off the meeting.

☞ **Set the purpose.** Ensure that parents know the purpose of the meeting before you begin the conversation, and set an expected duration. This can help to relax an anxious parent who may be fearing the worst.

☞ **Ask before taking notes.** Taking notes in the course of a conversation with a parent may not always be appropriate, but sometimes it is necessary! Checking at the outset that the parent is happy for you to do so creates a culture of mutual respect.

☞ **Summarise next steps.** Always end the meeting with a summary of action points and next steps – what the teacher or school will do next, and what the parent or carer is expected to do on their side.

Collaborative planning

The SEND Code of Practice is clear in its need for children with SEND to have a support plan in place that incorporates the views and input of all parties involved. Therefore the school, parents and pupil should agree on necessary adjustments, interventions and support, as well as the expected impact on progress, development or behaviour, along with a clear date for review. There is no formal requirement for this to be a written plan, although this does tend to be beneficial in ensuring that all involved have the same record and are pulling in the same direction for the child.

When planning children's provision with parents, it is important to recall the steps outlined above for running a successful SEND meeting. It is easy to get sidetracked by the needs and challenges that are being faced, but it is important to pay attention to wellbeing and emotional needs, to always start with pupil strengths, and to learn from what has worked well to date. A positive meeting can set the tone for positive collaboration moving forward. Always end any planning meeting with summary of next steps and action to be taken by all, as well as agreeing when you will next get together.

Homework support

For a parent of a child with attention and focus difficulties, motivating them to attend conscientiously to homework can be a huge challenge for all involved. It is also often an issue that can jeopardise the parent-school relationship, as parents can feel that the school is seeking to dictate what happens at home and thereby having a negative impact on home life. Homework can vary greatly from school to school depending on specific policies, and there may not be a huge amount of flexibility available to teachers. However, it is worth considering the following.

H²h How to help – homework
How to Help

☞ Ensure that homework is engaging, fun and clear. For a parent to successfully engage and support their child in homework, they must be clear on the expected outcome and the processes that need to take place. Provide a visual example of what is expected.

☞ Where possible, involve technology in order to give children with attention difficulties immediate feedback to support engagement.

☞ Support the process of getting the homework home and back to school in order for it to be acknowledged and valued. Remember, a generic class instruction to collect homework books, or get homework out of school bags and hand it in, may not be internalised or processed by pupils with attention difficulties. Have an established routine, visual reminders, personal reminders and a designated place to hand it in!

☞ Ensure that parents are aware of skills and adjustments used in class that can be replicated at home. Learning support strategies such as a quiet space without distractions, time limits, brain breaks and built-in movement can all be replicated at home if parents are aware of them.

☞ For some children, not doing their homework at home can be the best solution! Consider offering a homework club in school, or advise parents to have a different routine – perhaps taking homework to the local library after school on a Friday. That way, homework does not impinge on home life and it can become a more positive experience.

Reward systems and daily communication

As we have seen, children with attention difficulties can often be mis-labelled as inherently 'naughty', or as making poor behaviour choices. Often the same challenges seen in school are faced by parents outside school – but without the school's specialist toolkit for dealing with them! All children respond well to consistency, so support parents by sharing resources and ensuring that the systems that work in school are transferred, wherever possible, to the home environment. Sharing class reward and behaviour systems to replicate at home can also help parents to feel empowered.

Things always work best when school and home work collaboratively as a partnership, and this requires clear, open and honest communication. When children know that their school and their parents are talking and working together, they often respond much more positively to the support systems that are put in place. Some parents like to link school and home rewards, and to deal with them cumulatively. If this is the case, then needless to say they will need to know how the day has gone! Ideas for achieving this are:

■ **Home-school contact books.** These can be effective in sharing the achievements and challenges from the school day, so that they can be further reinforced at home, and vice versa. It is a permanent record of behaviour, so take care not to let it become a book of misdemeanours. If you do need to pass on negative feedback to parents, perhaps indicate that you will telephone at a later time. Engage the child in the passing of this book – it is a good transition object between home and school, and also encourages development of a sense of responsibility!

- **Traffic light systems.** These are a quick visual cue to parents as how the day has gone. This can either be one summative light, or a pattern across the day – again, involve the child in the decision making!
- **Verbal handovers.** Ensure that the child is part of these conversations, and that they overhear super-positive things about themselves!

As we have seen, pupils with ADHD are thought to receive 20,000 more negative messages during the course of their school years than their neurotypical peers. With this in mind, it is vital that communication between home and school is positive and purposeful. Establishing a regular positive check-in can be beneficial, especially if held in the child's presence and paired with tangible objects. For example, children can write all the good things they accomplish over a week on slips of paper and post them into a 'golden box'. At the end of the week this can be shared with parents, ensuring that successes rather than challenges are always the primary focus of the home-school relationship.

Chapter 18: Diagnosis and support

When faced with a child who is inattentive, lacks concentration, can't sit still and struggles to regulate their emotions in a school setting, teachers and other education professionals can often begin to look for those symptoms that fit the descriptors of ADHD or other neurodiverse conditions such as autism or dyslexia. It may therefore be the case, as we have noted, that the classroom teacher is the first professional to notice a child's attention, focus and processing difficulties, in addition to other tendencies and behaviours linked to these conditions – in other words, to identify patterns of behaviour and link them to a possible specific difficulty.

> ## Key Point
>
> *It may be the case that the classroom teacher is the first professional to notice a child's attention, focus and processing difficulties.*

As the SEND Code of Practice states, early identification of needs lead to the best outcomes for children. The route to diagnosis can be a long and difficult one, which needs to be approached with caution and care in order for all the necessary points on the journey to be reached without taking a wrong turn! For parents, hearing that their child faces challenges can be upsetting, frightening and worrying. At the same time, it can also be reinforcing, eye opening and a relief! It is therefore important that when discussing and addressing these issues that the approach taken is one of care and kindness.

When teachers are speaking to parents and broaching possible traits and patterns of behaviour that their children are displaying in school, it is often the case that the parents either wholeheartedly agree and reveal that they have been having the same thoughts and were just waiting for someone else to 'notice', or alternatively go through a very normal process of denial and personal affront at the very suggestion. The latter is obviously a more challenging outcome and needs to be addressed carefully. The best course of action is to give parents time to process, time to think and time to do their own research and speak to their families. It is ultimately a parent's final decision whether a referral for assessment takes place; the responsibility of the education professional is only ever to signpost and support.

Once on a referral pathway for a young person, it is important that teachers are fully supportive and understanding of parents through every stage, both during the waiting period and following an assessment and possible diagnosis. Waiting times can often be long and, as the only professionals that a parents can easily access, teachers can often bear the brunt of frustrations. It is important at such times to remember that this is not personal. For some parents, a possible diagnosis represents the distant end point of their journey – the final destination. However, it is of paramount importance that parents view diagnosis as only a fork in the road, a step on the way. Teachers have a vital role to play in supporting this understanding.

Unlike support plan discussions and general SEND meetings, once a referral pathway is in place the conversations that occur and the documents that surround them are often solely focused around the young person's problems and challenges, rather than on the balance of their strengths and difficulties. Such a development can feel very negative to a parent, and this needs to be supported and understood. Pre-warning a parent that this will be the case is one simple preventative measure that can reduce potential upset. When a child is due to be assessed, it can be a positive and supportive approach for the teacher to offer to attend the appointment with the parents. This shows solidarity, as well as giving the teacher an opportunity to learn more about the pupil in his or her care and to speak about the child from a perspective of what is seen within the school environment.

If the outcome of assessment is a diagnosis, then further support will be required – whatever the parents' reaction. Some parents express grief when their child is diagnosed with a specific difficulty, others denial. Either way, teachers as supportive professionals must let parents feel whatever they need to feel, and respond with care and kindness. It is important to ensure from the outset that any recommendations from medical professionals are shared with all staff working with the child, and that appropriate strategies and approaches are built into the child's support plan and reviewed regularly in partnership with the parents for impact and need to adjust.

It is vital for teachers to remember, when working with parents, that to be successful requires working as a team. Research from the Education Endowment Fund (EEF) echoes other studies in concluding that successful parental engagement and relationships can improve age-related outcomes for children. Working together, ensuring that everyone's voice is heard and listened to, and remembering that parents are the experts on and best advocates for their children, is always the surest route to success.

Parent support groups

Many schools have established systems
of parent workshops and support groups
covering a wide range of areas such as
managing childhood worries, supporting
children with emotional challenges,
and positive parenting. Setting up such
workshops or groups within a school can
offer parents a much needed outlet for
their frustrations and anxieties, as well as
giving them an opportunity to create links
and relationships with others who face
similar challenges. As we have said, parenting a child with ADHD can
be a lonely and isolating experience, and it can be hugely uplifting and
empowering for a parent to realise that they are not alone and their child
isn't the only one facing problems of this kind.

> ## *Key Point*
>
> *Support groups can
> provide parents with an
> outlet for their anxieties
> and an opportunity
> to create links with
> others who face
> similar challenges.*

Below we describe how a parent workshop might operate in practice.
However, a support group doesn't need to have any specific focus, and
it can simply be an opportunity for adults to gather together and work
collaboratively with or without the children. Having a regular slot in the
school week set aside for this makes it easy, as trying to recruit members
and set up meetings from scratch might prove to be an overwhelming
task. Once established, the group can be self-managed by parents and
work in a preventative capacity to empower and upskill, ultimately
supporting children and resulting in raised levels of wellbeing within
the classroom setting.

H²h How to help – parent support workshops
How to Help

Parent support workshops, involving parents along with their children, can work to support pupils with attention difficulties and can have a range of positive outcomes for the child, the parents and the family as a whole A collaborative approach can serve to strengthen bonds between parents and children by encouraging them to work together, often in a creative capacity, and it can also be restorative. Possible areas of focus might include:

☞ Creating a collaborative Home Charter of rules

☞ Creating a morning routine checklist

☞ Creating an emotional regulation scale to use at home

☞ Developing strategies to prevent emotional overload, such as Mindfulness or Growth Mindset strategies

☞ Developing further understanding of the child's condition

Chapter 19: The role of medication

Medication will always be a controversial issue where young people are concerned, whether the management of ADHD is involved or not, and deciding whether to go down this route is never an easy decision for a family to take. Medication should only be considered after thorough evaluation, and in circumstances where earnest attempts at non-medical intervention have proved insufficient, the child is at risk of academic failure or emotional damage and/or the child poses a significant risk to themselves and others. Despite this need to proceed with extreme caution, it is undeniably true to say that, when it works, medication can have very positive effects.

> ## Key Point
>
> *Despite the need to proceed with extreme caution, when it works, medication can have very positive effects.*

There are two main kinds of treatment for ADHD, which can broadly be classified as stimulants and non-stimulants. Stimulants include methylphenidate, dextroamphetamine and lisdexamfetamine. Non-stimulants include atomoxetine and guanfacine. These chemical descriptions indicate the active compounds involved; the drugs themselves are typically marketed and sold under brand names. For example Ritalin is methylphenidate, Dexedrine is dextroamphetamine, Vyvanse is lisdexamfetamine, Strattera is atomoxetine and Tenex is guanfacine. Other medication options sometimes considered in the treatment and management of ADHD include clonidine, risperidone, melatonin and some types of antidepressants.

Stimulants

Stimulants are thought to increase the levels of a chemical messenger called *dopamine* in the brain – this appears to reduce symptoms of hyperactivity and impulsivity, and to promote attentiveness. Methylphenidate is by far the most used stimulant option. It exists in short-acting forms lasting three to four hours and also long-acting forms which last for extended periods during the day. Possible side effects of methylphenidate include loss of appetite (a common but transient symptom), inability to sleep and a feeling of nervousness; headaches and stomach pains can also occur.

Non-stimulants

Non-stimulants work differently from stimulants. They increase the level of the brain's chemical messenger *noradrenaline*, thereby addressing ADHD symptoms for those for whom it is effective. Response to non-stimulants is usually within two weeks, but maximum effect may not occur until after six to eight weeks. Typical benefits of non-stimulants include a positive effect on mood and sleep, and a reduction in feelings of anxiety. Side effects can result in a lack of appetite and stomache ache, although this is often mild.

Evaluating suitability for medication

The process that must take place before a child can be prescribed medication for ongoing use is, needless to say, an extremely comprehensive and careful one. It can be summarised as follows:

- Observations of symptoms are made by teachers and parents.
- This information is passed to an educational psychologist or clinician.
- Assessment for and diagnosis of ADHD takes place.
- A structured learning environment is provided.
- Monitoring is carried out over an agreed period of time.
- Based on results, the decision is made to seek medication.
- A base rate is established to understand which medication in which dosage is likely to be most suitable for the child.
- The medication trial takes place.
- Any side effects are reported and necessary adjustments are made.
- The benefits of the medication are presented.
- The situation is evaluated.

All school staff involved in the care and education of the child should be fully aware of the medication trial, as their feedback will be critical. Looking out for and reporting side effects or any changes over time is essential to the process, and any signs of tics, withdrawal, odd behaviour or poor health should be reported immediately – even if the adult is unsure about the problem or is worried about being wrong. Teachers should also be aware that different medication formulations can be more or less effective at different ages and stages of a child's development.

For any medication, regular reviews are needed to establish how the child's ongoing development may affect the dose required, and to measure other indicators of normal health as well as any side effects of the medication.

Medication in practice

Monitoring the effect of a medication in addressing behaviour, and also any potential side effects, requires full cooperation between teachers, health professionals and parents. More broadly, teachers and support professionals should be aware that although medication is sometimes a very effective option, it is only one of several tools available for managing ADHD – and the decision whether or not to use it will partly depend on a judgement of benefits versus costs. Medication cannot 'cure' children with ADHD, but it may enable them to concentrate better, and thus to learn more effectively.

Key Point

Medication cannot 'cure' children with ADHD, but it may enable them to concentrate better, and thus to learn more effectively.

Few children with ADHD will actively enjoy taking medication, even though it may be helping them academically, behaviourally and socially. Some don't like to feel different, and may be embarrassed by other people (especially their peers) knowing that they take medicine. In addition, a minority of students may suffer from low-level side effects such as stomach upsets, especially in the early stages of treatment. The best way to handle these issues is for the child to meet with the supervising specialist, typically either a paediatrician or a psychiatrist, to review the situation and discuss options. Ideally, the child should be positive about this course of action. Once a course of treatment is in progress, any side effects can usually be eradicated by minor changes in dosage, or by changing the time when pills are taken.

For any child on medication, communication between the family, the health professional and the school is crucial. Although the final decision as to whether or not medication is prescribed rests with the health professional, the family and SENCO have essential roles to play in monitoring outcomes and reassuring the child about confidentiality within the school context. Indeed, parents may well discuss medication with an empathetic teacher or SENCO before they ever approach their GP. How, then, can school staff offer informed advice to parents, and guide them as they consider options?

How to help – medication facts for parents and carers

☞ While it needs to be used carefully and wisely, medication can be administered to children with ADHD safely and effectively.

☞ Medication can reduce extraneous activity and improve attention, self-control, handwriting, motivation and academic performance.

☞ Medication should always be considered as an option for children with significant difficulties caused by ADHD; there is currently significant under-medication in the UK.

☞ Medication is only one option available to assist children with ADHD, and should always be integrated with the core approaches of educational intervention and behaviour management.

☞ Medication does not make children into 'zombies'; stimulant medications are non-addictive and do not produce a 'high'.

☞ Fine-tuning of dosage in terms of both quantity and timing is essential for effective management, and combinations of medications may sometimes be necessary in complex cases.

☞ Parents and carers should look carefully into the rationale for using medication to manage ADHD, and the facts about side effects.

Chapter 20: Counselling, coaching and CBT

Changes in society have reduced the opportunities available to many young people to have someone with whom to discuss, formalise and clarify their thinking, especially those students with learning and behavioural difficulties. Providing such opportunities within school has been achieved informally through initiatives such as Circle Time and PSHE discussion, but for a child who needs more personal and individual support this assistance can be patchy. Increasing pressure has meant that teachers often do not have the time to implement individual responses and, many would argue, also lack the specific training and skills to undertake this task.

Counselling

Counselling is a process that assists individuals to focus on their concerns while simultaneously exploring problems, making choices, managing crises and working through feelings of conflict. It allows young people to gain a better understanding of themselves and the situations they encounter, as well as developing strategies to manage change. As a result, counselling in schools can be a cost-effective solution for pupils experiencing emotional distress and/or behavioural problems as a result of relationship difficulties, loss and anxiety.

> ### *Key Point*
> *Counselling assists individuals to focus on concerns while exploring problems, making choices, managing crises and working through feelings.*

When a pupil's emotional distress is left unaddressed, the resulting tension can lead to deterioration in attitude and mental stamina. This in turn can lead to truancy, lower school performance and disaffection. Emotional wellbeing is clearly correlated with ADHD, and it is not possible for a school to improve inclusion and learning outcomes without considering the impact of emotional stress on attainment.

Counselling is likely to benefit a pupil with ADHD who:

- Demonstrates extreme mood swings
- Shows indicators of school refusal
- Bullies or is bullied

- May have experienced abuse
- Displays emotional responses to stress e.g. self-harming, eating disorders

The purpose of counselling in a school context is to support pupils sufficiently to allow them to function effectively, access the curriculum and engage with the activities offered within school. It is important to make a distinction between general counselling-informed skills that may be used on an everyday basis by school staff, and the more formal process of counselling used by trained and qualified counsellors. It would be difficult in practice to combine the role of teacher with that of formal counsellor as the two may conflict in a number of ways – for example discipline and parent liaison. The need to establish equality of status between counsellor and client can also lead to problems when the two roles are combined, in addition to which highly sensitive issues may arise. For a combination of these reasons, most schools employ or 'buy-in' qualified and accountable professional counsellors.

Counselling can take several forms, but increasingly popular approach is 'brief counselling', Brief counselling fits well with the time constraints of school-based intervention, and is aimed at 'enabling' the pupil. In a sense, it represents a 'quick fix' rather than the deeper process of reconstruction involved in full psychodynamic therapy. In some cases as few as two or three sessions can lead to improvements for specific pupils, although if the aim is to change both behaviour and emotional responses then it is likely that more sessions will be required.

Finding the right type of person to provide a counselling service is not easy: often both students and staff may be somewhat suspicious, and it can be an especially difficult process for pupils who already struggle to develop relationships. Other issues that need to be addressed include:

- Provision of an environment that allows pupils to feel secure enough to expose their feelings
- Resources
- Timetable constraints
- Ensuring that aims and techniques are consistent with school ethos
- Ensuring that counselling styles respond to pupil needs

In practice, as it becomes clear that counselling is having a positive effect on the behaviour and attitude of specific children, both students and staff tend to come to recognise its value to the school community.

Coaching

For many people, the terms 'coaching' and 'mentoring' are interchangeable, but it is important to distinguish between the two. Mentoring is usually considered to be an activity that takes place on a one to one basis, with one person being the leader and the other the learner. By contrast, coaching is a collaboration of equal partners in order to achieve shared aims. While coaching often takes place on an individual basis, groups can also be coached.

> ## *Key Point*
>
> *Coaching in a classroom context focuses on improving learning outcomes for all by providing greater focus on and awareness of choice.*

Coaching in a classroom context focuses on improving learning outcomes for all by providing greater focus on and awareness of choice. It looks at the stage each pupil is at today and encourages shared responsibility to achieve where they want to be tomorrow by acquiring the skills necessary for progress. Coaching supports improvement in specific areas; in schools, it is most effective when there is a clear agenda of items that are central to the performance of the individuals within the school.

Coaching can support individuals with ADHD by:

- Developing knowledge and skills
- Engendering trust and responsibility
- Providing a supportive culture

In a school that facilitates a coaching approach during lessons, the teachers and teaching assistants encourage verbal interaction amongst learners and use this as a springboard to encourage them to contribute observations and explore ideas further. This creates discussion, leads to greater clarity and moves learning forward. Risk-taking behaviour is encouraged, and pupils come to understand that incorrect responses are valued as much as correct ones for their role in developing understanding. Coaching therefore fosters environments where all pupils feel secure and able to partake in discussions, safe in the knowledge that their views will always be valued.

Coaching techniques can only be successful in a classroom setting if seen as part of a strategic intervention that aims to increase the success of all, rather than a way of supporting a specific individual's needs. It requires the support of the whole organisation, and may demand a significant amount of preparation work to ensure that skills and attitudes are conducive to its application. Coaching requires trust, as relationships are paramount to its success. It also requires a considerable investment of time in order to provide training, implementation and opportunities for reflection and evaluation.

In order to be effective coaches within a school environment, staff need to be supported to develop a number of underpinning skills including:

- Communication and interpersonal skills
- Creative thinking skills
- Active listening skills
- Reflective and open questioning skills
- The ability to facilitate confidence in others and oneself to make mistakes and see these as learning opportunities
- The ability to motivate others to achieve aims
- Being comfortable with ambiguity and disagreement

Cognitive behavioural therapy (CBT)

Cognitive behavioural therapy was developed forty years ago by pioneers including Aaron Beck, and has proven to be effective in treating anxiety, depression and behaviour problems. Research suggests that it works better than other forms of therapy for ADHD[39], although most professionals do not advocate that it should replace an effective medication regime altogether. Indeed, a study led by Professor Steven Safren at Massachusetts General Hospital found that a combination of medication and CBT was more effective at controlling ADHD symptoms than medication alone.[40]

Expert View

"CBT picks up where medication leaves off."

Steven A. Safren

Results can be achieved relatively quickly; traditional forms of therapy such as psychoanalysis can go on for years, but CBT typically yields its benefits within just twelve to fifteen one-hour sessions. The focus is on looking at ways in which the transient thoughts and enduring beliefs that

---

39 Sherman, C., Ramsay, J.R., & Barrow, K. (2021). *How CBT Dismantles ADHD Negativity: Cognitive Behavioral Therapy Overview*. ADDitude. Accessed at https://www.additudemag.com/cognitive-behavioral-therapy-for-adhd/

40 Safren, S. et al. (2010). Cognitive behavioral therapy vs relaxation with educational support for medication-treated adults with ADHD and persistent symptoms: a randomized controlled trial. *Journal of the American Medical Association* 304 (8), 875-880.

we hold about ourselves affect how we feel and act. From a perspective of attention difficulties, CBT is a powerful tool for getting organised, staying focused, and improving one's ability to manage emotions and get along with other people.

How to help – understanding CBT

CBT teaches ways to recognise distorted thoughts in order to replace them with more realistic alternatives. Unhelpful patterns of thinking that can be address with cognitive behavioural therapy might include:

☞ **All or nothing thinking.** You view everything as entirely good or entirely bad: if you don't do something perfectly, you've failed.

☞ **Over-generalisation.** You see a single negative event as part of a pattern: for example, you think you always forget to pay your bills.

☞ **Mind reading.** You believe that you know what other people think about you or something you've done — and it's always bad.

☞ **Fortune telling.** You are certain that things will turn out badly.

☞ **Magnification and minimisation.** You exaggerate the significance of minor problems while trivialising your accomplishments.

☞ **'Should' statements.** You focus on how things should be, leading to severe self-criticism and feelings of resentment toward others.

☞ **Personalisation.** You blame yourself for negative events and downplay the role and responsibility of others.

☞ **Mental filtering.** You see only the negative aspects of any experience, and filter out the positive aspects.

☞ **Emotional reasoning.** You assume that your negative feelings reflect reality, when in reality they do not.

☞ **Comparative thinking.** You measure yourself against others and feel inferior, even though the comparison may be unrealistic.

Chapter 21: Sleep, exercise and nutrition

Sleep

Children of different ages require different amounts of sleep. The American Academy of Sleep Medicine (AASM) produced a 'Consensus Statement' in 2016 regarding recommended amount of sleep for paediatric populations.[41] The figures below gives an indication of the amount of sleep children of different ages require on a regular basis to promote optimal health:

- Infants 4 to 12 months: 12-16 hours of sleep, including naps
- Children 1 to 2 years: 11-14 hours of sleep, including naps
- Children 3 to 5 years: 10-13 hours of sleep, including naps
- Children 6 to 12 years: 9-12 hours of sleep
- Teenagers 13 to 18 years: 8-10 hours of sleep

Almost three in every four children and adolescents with ADHD issues also have a sleep disorder. Not getting enough sleep, or needing to sleep at times that don't fit with school or work obligations, can have significant long-term effects including physical illness, behavioural issues and mood changes. While it may be obvious that an adult is tired when they are behind on sleep, fatigue in children often looks like exaggerated ADHD symptoms: hyperactivity, impulsivity, and sometimes even aggressiveness or 'acting out'.

> ## *Key Point*
>
> *Almost three in every four children and adolescents who have ADHD issues also have a sleep disorder.*

For young children with ADHD, it can be difficult to settle at the end of the day. Perhaps the child is wound up from the day's events and can't stop talking, or perhaps they are so absorbed in a book or a puzzle that they don't want to stop reading to brush their teeth and put on their pyjamas. Although these are not in themselves troubling behaviors, when they occur every night they can frustrate both the child and the parents, and this frustration can in turn further interfere with sleep habits.

The main option available for children and young people with sleep issues is good 'sleep hygiene'. This involves day-to-day things that can

---

41   Paruthi S. et al. (2016). Recommended amount of sleep for pediatric populations: a consensus statement of the AASM. Journal of Clinical Sleep Medicine 12(6): 785–786.

be done at home to promote good quality sleep such as having fixed bedtimes, keeping the bedroom comfortable, and relaxing as bedtime approches. Caffeine in carbonated drinks, coffee and chocolate, eating a heavy meal, exercising and taking stimulant medications can all affect sleep to varying degrees, and should be avoided late in the day.

Having a bedtime routine and a set bedtime can help a child to understand what to expect and how they should behave. A routine can start thirty minutes to two hours before bedtime, and can include winding down activities such as a warm bath or reading a story. Sticking to a set pattern each night will help your child to settle and give them the time to calm down before sleeping. Going to the toilet as the very last task before getting into bed can also help prevent them from needing to get up in the night.

The use of electronic devices such as televisions, mobile phones and tablet computers close to bedtime can prevent children from settling to sleep. This is because they produce light that is good at suppressing the natural hormones in the brain that cause sleepiness. Ideally, these devices should not be used in the hours before bed, and should be removed from the child's bedroom in order to create an environment that the child associates with sleep. If your child currently uses these devices to help them fall asleep, consider replacing this routine with a bedtime story or soothing music.

One further option is melatonin. This is a naturally occurring hormone produced by the brain that is involved in managing a person's biological 'body clock' and helping to regulate sleep patterns. A melatonin product, called Circadin, may be licensed for use from your GP. It can only be obtained on prescription and comes in the form of a 'prolonged-release' tablet. Prolonged-release means that the drug treatment continues working over a number of hours as the active ingredient is released slowly into the body.

Exercise

Exercise isn't just good for toning muscles; it's also essential for keeping the brain in shape. Studies have shown that children with ADHD who exercise perform better on tests of attention and have less impulsivity than those who do not,[42,43] and exercise helps the brain to release dopamine which can support attention and concentration. As the stimulant medicines used to treat ADHD work by increasing the amount of dopamine, it is important that exercise is part of every well-rounded ADHD treatment plan, and that a number of supporting options are used to facilitate this process.

Scientists believe that exercise works on children's brains in several ways:

- **Blood flow.** Exercise increases blood flow to the brain. Children with ADHD may have less blood flow to the parts of their brain that are responsible for thinking, planning, emotions and behaviour.
- **Blood vessels.** Exercise improves blood vessels and brain structure. This helps with thinking ability, as the increased blood flow will enable greater brain function.
- **Brain activity.** Exercise increases activity in those parts of the brain related to behaviour and attention.

The 'wake and shake' sessions offered by many schools are a great way to get the blood pumping – and have fun! Caution is needed when building exercise into team sports, however, as many children with ADHD struggle with fine and gross motor skills and social interactions. As a result, they do not excel in competitive group activities and care must to be taken not to simply set up yet another area where they do not succeed.

Health experts recommend that children should get at least sixty minutes of moderate to intense exercise every day. How they get it doesn't really matter – it might be cycling, swimming, running, football, dancing or any number of other things. Indeed, there is evidence that simply getting outside and spending time in the open air can 'calm the storm' in some children with ADHD. In one study, a short walk in the park helped children with ADHD to concentrate more effectively than an urban walk.[44]

42   Chang Y., Liu S., Yu H. & Lee Y. (2012). Effect of acute exercise on executive function in children with attention deficit hyperactivity disorder. *Archives of Clinical Neuropsychology* 27 225–237.

43   Mahon A.D. et al. (2013). Acute exercise effects on measures of attention and impulsivity in children with ADHD. *Journal of Educational and Developmental Psychology.* 3(2):65.

44   University of Illinois at Urbana-Champaign. *A Walk In The Park Improves Attention In Children With ADHD.* ScienceDaily. 15 October 2008.

Nutrition

A good diet is important to humans and other animals not only for physical health, but also for optimal mental development and functioning. Nutrition can affect one's mood, behaviour and capacity to learn – at home, at school and in the workplace. Having said this, the importance of diet to ADHD can be overstated. For many years diet was portrayed as a major factor in ADHD symptoms; however, research has shown that only 5% of children with ADHD respond to particular substances in their diet in a direct and obvious way.[45]

While the exact mechanisms by which diet may or may not interact with the symptoms of ADHD are still being debated, what is not in doubt is that healthy eating with a good variety of nutritional foods that provide a constant blood sugar level throughout the day is beneficial for all pupils. Children who live in a chaotic home, perhaps with a parent who also has a degree of ADHD, may not be provided with a particularly nourishing breakfast or lunchbox, and this can only exacerbate their difficulties.

Highly unsaturated fatty acids (HUFA)

Omega-3 and Omega-6 fatty acids are found in fish and seafood, in some nuts and seeds, and in green leafy vegetables. They are critical for normal brain development and function, but they are often lacking from modern diets. Everyone needs adequate dietary supplies of these highly unsaturated fatty acids (HUFA) for mental and physical health, but research shows that some people may need higher levels in their diet than others.[46] Factors that might lead to an increased need for HUFA in the diet could include:

■ Difficulties in the conversion of simple essential fatty acids (EFA) into the more complex Omega-3 and Omega-6 HUFA that the brain needs.

■ Unusually rapid breakdown and loss of these HUFA.

■ Difficulties in recycling, transporting or incorporating HUFA into cell membranes.

There is some evidence for each of these factors in children with ADHD, dyslexia, developmental coordination disorder (DCD, or dyspraxia), and autism, and HUFA supplements may therefore help in the management of these conditions. Controlled trials have provided preliminary evidence for

---

45 Hjalmarsdottir, F. (2020). Does nutrition play a role in ADHD? Healthline. Accessed at https://www.healthline.com/nutrition/nutrition-and-adhd

46 Lands, B. (2017). Highly unsaturated fatty acids (HUFA) mediate and monitor food's impact on health. *Prostaglandins and Other Lipid Mediators, 133: 4-10.*

this in ADHD and dyslexia, but further trials are still needed, especially with respect to developmental coordination disorder and autism. Research indicates that while both Omega-3 and Omega-6 fatty acids are important for optimal brain function, and that of the Omega-3 fatty acids eicosapentaenoic acid (EPA) is likely to be more beneficial than docosahexaenoic acid (DHA).[47]

The picture will continue to unfold but, at present, the balanced view seems to be that Omega oil supplements may provide some improvement in brain functioning but not to the same degree as established treatments such as stimulants. Also, when given with stimulants, there may be an additive effect of making fits more likely in a susceptible child. More broadly, it is essential to remember that ADHD, dyslexia, DCD and autism are not static conditions but descriptive labels for particular patterns of behavioural and learning difficulties. In practice, the differences within these conditions are significant, and many individuals show features of more than one condition.

Water

One area that is without dispute in terms of behaviour and learning is the benefit of good hydration. Mental performance can fall by as much as 10% when children are not adequately hydrated. Thirst will also add to tiredness, headaches and irritability for all children, and good hydration is therefore particularly important for children with ADHD who will have a lower threshold for all of these issues. Frequent small intakes of water are better for learning than limiting drinks to breaks and lunchtimes. Ideally, children need to drink eight glasses of water throughout the course of a day.

---

47 Dyall, S.C. (2015). Long-chain omega-3 fatty acids and the brain: a review of the independent and shared effects of EPA, DPA and DHA. *Frontiers in Aging Neuroscience*, 7: 52.

H²h How to help – diet and ADHD
How to Help

Scientific research regarding the impact of diet on ADHD is limited and the results are mixed. Many experts, however, do believe that diet may have a role to play in relieving ADHD symptoms. Brain researcher and ADHD expert Daniel Amen, MD, recommends these ADHD diet suggestions:[48]

☞ Eat a high-protein diet including beans, cheese, eggs, meat, and nuts. Add protein foods in the morning and for after-school snacks, to improve concentration and possibly increase the time for medication to work.

☞ Eat fewer simple carbohydrates such as sweets, honey, sugar, white flour products, white rice, and potatoes without the skins.

☞ Eat more complex carbohydrates such as vegetables and some fruits (including oranges, pears, grapefruit, apples and kiwi fruit). Eating complex carbohydrates at night may aid sleep.

☞ Eat more Omega-3 fatty acids such as those found in tuna, salmon, walnuts, Brazil nuts, and olive and canola oil. Omega-3 fatty acids are also available as supplements.

---

48 Amen, D.G. (2020). 9 Foods to Supercharge Your Brain Health. ADDitude. Accessed at https://www.additudemag.com/slideshows/adhd-nutrition-brain/

Chapter 22: ICT and Speech and Language Therapy

ICT

Information and communications technology (ICT) is a constantly developing area, and one where children and young people with ADHD are often able to find a non-threatening environment within which to achieve success. For many among them, learning has become associated with the fear of failure, both in their own eyes and in the eyes of those around them. The computer (in any of its manifestations) can provide a neutral setting within which to experiment, with students confident that they are controlling the pace and the level of work. In addition, as some learners with ADHD find it hard to establish relationships and don't always easily relate to other people, using a computer can avoid this problem and offer an entry point for another person to join in alongside them in a non-threatening manner.

> ### *Key Point*
>
> *ICT is an area where children and young people with ADHD are often able to find a non-threatening environment within which to achieve success.*

Having said this, it's important to acknowledge that multimedia options can also be problematic for risk-takers in terms of use of inappropriate sites, indulging in extensive and reckless online shopping and so on. The issue of cyberbullying is also something that youngsters must be aware of and able to deal with. Careful monitoring and once again a balance of structure and flexibility are essential. However the benefits outweigh the costs, and overall technology can be an asset for those with ADHD – whose frequent difficulties with time management, organisation and attention to detail can make it difficult for them to stay on task in a school or work environment.

There is a vast array of ICT equipment to help students with ADHD. Devices such as handheld spellcheckers and calculators can support learners who have difficulties with sequencing and memorising. Electronic timers can help students stay on task and pace themselves as they work. And multimedia technologies, which can present sounds, photographs and video as well as text on the screen, provide new directions for working with all students who may have learning and behaviour difficulties. These technologies are motivating and 'cool', and present opportunities for pupils to demonstrate what has been learned in ways that are less dependent on the written word. In addition, apps and computer programs can help people with ADHD to stay organised, reach goals, and even fight the urge to succumb to distraction.

Overall, when used properly, digital tools can help people with ADHD to improve their focus, increase their productivity, and remember to hand their work in on time. However, for parents to prevent technology from taking over, it is important to delegate media-free times (e.g. mealtimes, celebrations) and media-free zones (e.g. bedrooms, outdoor spaces) to set limits on media use. More broadly, the use of technology requires balance and self-monitoring. It should be utilised in two directions – to help increase productivity, but also to help decrease distraction and hyper-focus.

Despite the common mindset that technology has caused a generation of children to lack attention, there is actually very little evidence to justify this. In fact, a recent paper published by the Psychiatry and Behavioural Learning Network[49] outlined how the US Food and Drug Administration (FDA) has cleared a video game as a prescription treatment for children with ADHD. The 'EndeavorRx' app is a digital treatment indicated to improve attention function, as measured by computer-based testing, in children aged between eight and twelve with primarily inattentive or combined-type ADHD and a demonstrated attention issue.

The FDA clearance was based on data from five clinical studies spanning more than six hundred children with ADHD that showed EndeavorRx to be beneficial in improving objective measures of attention. A third of children no longer had a measurable deficit on at least one objective measure of attention after a month of using the app, and nearly half of all parents involved with the study reported a clinically meaningful change in their child's day-to-day impairments. After a second month, the proportion reporting change increased to 68%, and the improvements were maintained for up to one month after use of the digital treatment ceased.

EndeavorRx will be available with a prescription in the USA and will be released as the centrepiece of the Endeavour Care Program, which includes the Endeavour treatment and a mobile tracking app and personal support services for caregivers. Can you imagine a future scenario where parents are complaining at their children to "get on that video game!!"?

---

49 Canady, V. (2020). FDA approves first video game Rx treatment for children with ADHD. Mental Health Weekly. Accessed at https://doi.org/10.1002/mhw.32423.

Speech and Language Therapy

Speech and language therapists (SLTs) are specialists in communication disorders who can help children experiencing a range of needs from mild to severe learning difficulties, dyslexia, developmental coordination disorder (DCD, or dyspraxia) and autism. Speech and language therapists work to assess, diagnose and develop a programme of care to maximise the communication potential of the people referred to them. In order to help an individual function to the best of their ability, an SLT may work directly with a child with ADHD who may have overlapping language issues but who may also lack skills in appropriate social language use. The reason for this is that many studies show that children with ADHD are at risk of articulation issues that affect their ability to produce letter sounds appropriate for their age.

> ## *Key Point*
>
> *SLTs work to assess, diagnose and develop a programme of care to maximise the communication potential of the people referred to them.*

Beyond this, children with ADHD also commonly have differences in fluency and vocal quality when speaking. They may produce more vocal repetitions or word fillers as they try to organise their thoughts, somewhat like a stammer. This can lead to impatience and misunderstandings from others, especially peers and siblings who generally don't have the same patience and perspective as adults. Children with ADHD process language differently and, because of their distractibility and related symptoms, they are more likely to stray off-topic when speaking. They also frequently struggle to find the right words, and to put their thoughts together quickly and in a linear fashion during conversations. Errors in grammar as they compose sentences may also occur, because of planning difficulties that may be present even when underlying skills in this area are intact.

All these ADHD-related symptoms, with or without actual language delays, may impact an individual's ability to communicate effectively. As one teacher put it: "Marian is like a computer without the printer attached. She has all the information in her head, but she can't give me the words in the right order as a hard copy."

Listening comprehension can also be a problem for students with ADHD, in particular because of difficulties in handling rapidly spoken language or trying to focus in distracting environments like a noisy classroom. It really is important that teachers in particular try to understand how a child with ADHD is trying to interpret the world around them, because although they may have the skills and interest to be involved in what is going on in the classroom they may miss key words and details. After a while, this may cause them to appear bored and non-compliant as they simply cannot access what is going on around them.

Trying to stay on task and focus is difficult enough for a child with ADHD; being in a classroom with a large group of other students brings further challenges. This is one reason why many children with ADHD often do better in one-to-one situations, and also a reason why misunderstandings happen and people say things like: "they can concentrate when they want to." This simply is not true; its just that there are fewer distractions. In fact, group situations can cause significant difficulties as students with ADHD may be challenged by multiple distractions and may not always be able to adhere to the classroom protocol of putting their hand up and waiting to be asked.

An example of this is provided by Jacob. He was a very enthusiastic twelve year old boy with ADHD who blurted out answers to questions during classes. Despite positive and negative prompting to wait his turn whenever he knew an answer, he always shouted out to the annoyance of other students and his teacher. When asked why, he said that unless he said his answer out loud straight away he would forget it. After discussion, it was agreed that Jacob wouldn't shout out his answers but instead would write them on a Post-it note along with the time. When he had ten notes he would take them to the teacher's desk – which also gave him a much-needed seat break.

In this way, the teacher was able get Jacob's answers without disrupting the class. This is a good example of the fact that, often, the first step to finding a solution to a problem of this kind is for the teacher to understand the individual rhythms of a specific student's work.

How to help – speech and language therapy

When looking to support children with ADHD using speech and language therapy, the key is to look for potential language delays and intervene when needed. Some suggestions for this might include:

☞ Evaluate for specific delays through direct testing, then initiate appropriate interventions when indicated.

☞ Wait until you gain a child's full attention before making a request or starting a conversation; otherwise, details may be missed. Help transition their attention by using a brief marker, such as "Ryan, I have a question for you", and try to maintain eye contact.

☞ Address pragmatic concerns for children struggling socially.

☞ Offer 'extended time' in conversation, allowing children who may be struggling to put all their thoughts together. Give them time to settle themselves and organise their responses.

☞ Pause often and parse language into short segments when speaking to someone with ADHD. Communicate clearly, and use gestures such as counting bullet points on your fingers. Rephrase or repeat when needed, and have children restate what they've understood.

Chapter 23: Transitions

Transitioning from one overarching life situation to another can present challenges for any young person. Familiar surroundings, faces and routines must be left behind, and new ones must be welcomed and accommodated. For someone with ADHD, the process of transition can be particularly problematic. Teachers and parents therefore need to make themselves aware of the issues and how to support the child or young person through a period of change, and training programmes for teachers and teaching assistants should address the characteristics of effective transition management.

Key Point

Transitions can present challenges for any young person; for someone with ADHD, the process of transition can be particularly problematic.

Early years to primary school transition

Moving from a less structured and more play-oriented environment to the more formalised setting of the classroom can potentially be both beneficial and problematic for children with ADHD. The open, less structured environment of early years education may have suited the ADHD impulsive learning style, but the potential for accidents and incidents may have already led to the child with ADHD acquiring a 'reputation' amongst teachers, peers and the parents of other children. As a result, the more structured classroom environment may provide an opportunity to apply the rules, rituals and routines that are especially needed by children with ADHD.

However, most important of all – and most difficult to achieve – is the acceptance by other members of the class and their parents of a child who may be seen as disruptive and difficult, but who is essentially just 'different'. It is likely that a degree of social exclusion will already have taken place before the primary school years begin: play-dates, party and sleepover invitations may not have been received by the child with ADHD, leading to a loss of self-esteem and confidence both for the individual and for his or her family. Wherever possible, it is advised that during school PHSE, Circle Time or Circle of Friends sessions, opportunities should be taken to explore neurodiversity and the differences of individuals within an inclusive community.

Primary to secondary school transition

One of the most important decisions to be made about a child's education involves the choice of secondary school. For parents of a child with ADHD, this is especially challenging. They will look for a secondary school that can offer a level of understanding and continuity of structure similar to that provided by a successful primary school, and this can be a very difficult quest. Time and time again, parental hopes and aspirations have been dashed by the huge differences that exist between primary and secondary settings. Parents need to be aware of what can reasonably be expected, how they can differentiate between schools, and the key criteria to use in making their choice. The primary school SENCO has a crucial role to play in this process, ensuring that parents are well-informed and able to ask appropriate questions with respect to the most relevant issues.

> ## Key Point
>
> *Time and time again, parental hopes and aspirations have been dashed by the huge differences that exist between primary and secondary settings.*

It is very difficult for a SENCO to predict the outcomes of transition to a specific secondary school by an individual student. What the glossy school brochure says the school can do, and what it really can do, will very much depend on the attitudes of the Head Teacher, Senior Management Team and Governors regarding special educational needs in general and ADHD in particular. However, establishing good links with neighbouring schools and colleagues will provide an insight into school policies and management, and help to determine how flexible they can be with students with ADHD. While a good indication of a secondary school's ability to provide stability and a caring ethos is happy staff and a low turnover of personnel, perhaps the single most important factor for parents of young people with ADHD is the attitude, experience and status of the SENCO, and how much influence they exert in relation to teaching, learning and behavioural policies across the school. This will often determine the approach of the rest of the staff.

How to help – choosing a secondary school

☞ Key factors to consider when choosing the right secondary school for a young person with ADHD include:

- The attitude of the Head Teacher, Senior Management Team and Governors with respect to ADHD.
- How the school deals with issues of organisational skills, differentiation of classwork, homework and non-structured time for students with ADHD.
- The school's attitude to working with external agencies.

☞ Key factors to consider when evaluating a secondary school SENCO and the responsibilities of their role include:

- Do they have experience of supporting other children with ADHD in the school?
- What arrangements are in place for supporting children with ADHD with issues of organisation, homework, making friends and so on?
- How does the school communicate with parents?
- Who does the parent contact if they have information that they wish to pass on?
- What arrangements are in place if the child needs to take medication?
- How does the school find out if a child has not taken his or medication as expected, and what action do they take?

Transition to further education or the workplace

Moving from school into university, college, training or the workplace is an exciting time. However for many young people, and especially those with ADHD, it can also be very traumatic. A change of routine is never easy for anyone, and it is doubly difficult for individuals who depend more than most on structure and familiar circumstances. Having said this, the opportunities to focus on specific subjects or to follow a skills-based approach to employment can work extremely well for individuals with ADHD who have found school difficult and possibly boring, and who may have had negative experiences with teaching staff.

The most important principle will be to direct young adults with ADHD towards academic courses, training or apprenticeships that best fit their personalities and abilities. This may involve a lot of research and sifting through course requirements and descriptions – something that students with ADHD may need a lot of help with. The opportunity to talk through possibilities, 'think out loud' and weigh up pros and cons of various routes will be invaluable. This is where a knowledgeable, trusted adult can make all the difference, and it does not necessarily have to be a parent; another family member, a teacher, a mentor or an older student can also fill the role.

How to help – next steps beyond school

☞ Key factors to contend with and adapt to for students with ADHD considering further education include:

- More independence and less dependence
- Self-organisation and planning for study
- Possibility of living away from home
- Budgeting resources and planning of time
- Socialisation and friendships

☞ Key factors to explore in terms of study and lifestyle support within a further education institution include:

- Make use of study support centres and wellbeing services
- Use the resources available to support your ADHD traits
- Get into a routine of going to all scheduled classes
- Work first and play later
- Use a calendar and get organised
- Join a club in order to meet new friends
- Think about and practise effective sleep and diet routines
- Use medication as prescribed and seek out options for renewals of prescriptions
- Contact your parents regularly – and not just for financial support

☞ Key risk factors to plan for when moving into a workplace include:

- Disorganisation and problems with prioritisation
- Poor planning and/or time management skills
- Problems focusing on a task
- Excessive activity or restlessness
- Low frustration tolerance and mood swings
- Problems following through and completing tasks
- Difficulty coping with stress

Part 5: ADHD at home

Chapter 24: Parenting a family with ADHD

As we bumble along on our journey of being a parent, we are often bombarded with well-meaning advice as to how to go about it. The truth is that every parent, child and family is different – no one parenting approach works consistently for every child all the time, a strategy that works for a while may later become less effective, and comparing oneself to others is likely to be meaningless or even counterproductive. So if you are the parent of a child with ADHD, or of a child who you suspect may have ADHD, please approach this section with an appropriate mindset. It is a compendium of ideas, wisdom and advice drawn from professional and personal experience, not a set of recipes for how to manage your unique child with his or her own individual strengths, challenges and personality.

When you first find yourself parenting a child with ADHD, it is common to experience feelings of grief and loss alongside a range of other, frequently conflicting emotions. However, it is vital that you do not waste precious time or energy blaming yourself. Questioning if the diagnosis is your fault, wondering if going about things differently when the child was a baby might have changed matters, or regretting not following Aunt Glenda's homespun advice about sleep and weaning – these are all pointless activities. ADHD is a form of neurodiversity and, as we have seen, in most cases it is inherited. Yes, it is possible for aspects of a home environment to make the symptoms of ADHD harder to manage – but alone they cannot cause ADHD in a child.

Throughout Part 5 of this book, we will explore a range of challenges that parents of children with ADHD commonly face throughout their years of child raising. In our careers we have been fortunate to work closely with many parents – and some of them have been kind enough to share their thoughts, fears, experiences and feelings with us. We will draw upon these real-life examples, reflecting a range of social backgrounds, genders and ages, to show that, despite stark contrasts in family set-up and context, the challenges and barriers faced by families with ADHD tend to be frighteningly similar. We will look a little deeper into the causes of these challenges, explore ways in which families seek to respond with varying levels of success, and describe practical strategies and ideas for how to help.

_H2h_ How to help – ADHD is nobody's fault
How to Help

☞ ADHD is a neurodiverse condition involving differences in certain areas of the brain – do not waste precious energy blaming yourself or the quality of your parenting for your child's difficulties.

☞ ADHD is often inherited, and it may be the case that when a child receives a diagnosis of ADHD the parent begins to see that they have faced a lifetime of similar challenges themselves.

☞ If this happens, the parent can take the first steps towards their own assessment and possible diagnosis by visiting their GP.

Let's meet the families

We are immensely grateful for the openness and honesty shown to us by seven mothers, whose insights into the experience of parenting sons and daughters with ADHD and comorbid conditions we are – thanks to their generosity – able to share with you in this part of the book. They are:

- Faye, mother to Belle, age 10.

  Belle is on the waiting list for an ADHD assessment. Her social challenges came to the fore when she joined KS2 and the playground became a _"more and more stressful"_ place.

- Fiona, mother to Matt, age 24.

  Fiona reflects on Matt's experiences on his journey to becoming a qualified prototype mechanic with Ford.

- Louise, mother to Emily, age 9.

  Emily was diagnosed at the age of 6 with moderate combined type ADHD.

- Amy, mother to Harry, age 9.

  Harry has received a diagnosis of ADHD combined with Autism Spectrum Disorder (ASD).

- Sheila, mother to Martin, age 31.

  Martin is now a police officer; Sheila shares her experiences from his childhood and teenage years.

■ We also spoke to two more mothers who asked to remain anonymous. Therefore, we shall give their children names as follows:

  ▓ Joe is 7 and has very recently received a diagnosis of combined type ADHD after a two year wait.

  ▓ William is 13 and has ADHD and sensory processing challenges.

The early days

From the moment that a pregnancy is announced, and with it the imminent arrival of a brand-new human being, all that we seem to see and hear are words – always given with the best intentions. Our shelves and fireplaces are adorned with congratulations cards, our bookshelves are stacked with parenting manuals and guides (which the babies have not read!), and in the earliest days we are surrounded by a wealth of support from friends, family, midwives and health visitors.

Unfortunately, few of these guests bring the truth along with their flowers, toys and sleepsuits. Despite the avalanche of words and information – and the constant rosy glow of our friends' seemingly perfect lives on social media – we are often not told that parenting is the hardest thing that any of us will ever do! Parenting is magical, rewarding, exciting and fun... and it is also exhausting, confusing and overwhelming. Add to that the additional load of parenting a child with ADHD, and these extremes can be magnified.

Self-care

For a child with ADHD, their parent is often their voice, their fighter, their advocate and their safe place – and to be all these things to a dependent human being can be exhausting. Self-care is therefore vital. We have all heard aircraft safety briefings saying that, in the event of an emergency, adults should fit their own oxygen mask before helping a child to fit theirs. This philosophy seems to go against all our maternal and paternal instincts, yet it is vital in ensuring that the parents of children with ADHD are able to provide everything that is required of them. You can't pour from an empty cup – and children with ADHD are going to be 'drinking' a great deal from your parenting cup – so be sure to meet your own needs first!

A child who needs regulating requires a well-regulated adult to help them, and as a parent you will be the adult who is the most trusted, the most reliable, and the most accessible. So be prepared to offer a lot of support! This is draining and tiring, so ensure that self-care is always top of your list of priorities. Try your hardest to be well-fed, well-rested and well-hydrated at all times, and you will know that you are in the best possible state of body and mind to be all the things that your child needs you to be.

How to help – becoming your child's safe place

☞ As the mother, father or carer of a child with ADHD, you will be your child's safe place – this is wonderful, but also emotionally turbulent and exhausting.

☞ The feelings of love and safety that primary caregivers give to their children can invite children with SEND to take out the most painful, difficult-to-manage emotions upon their parents – in other words, to use them as an emotional dumping ground.

☞ At these times, remind yourself that your child needs an outlet to release these emotions, and they will turn to the one they love the most. In other words, this is a parenting win!

☞ So when you are faced with a child who is finding life a challenge, and they dump all that negative emotion at your feet, sweep it up and hold it close – they are saying that they love you and feel safe with you.

Learn, learn, learn!

Once you have covered the self-care element of being a parent of a child with ADHD, the next important hurdle in supporting yourself, your child and your family is learning as much as possible about ADHD. Forewarned is forearmed! Learn as much as you can about ADHD itself, about your child, and about the specifics of your child with ADHD. At the same time, do not agonise over whether a given behaviour on a given day may or may not be driven by ADHD. Sometimes your child will just act like a typical child, and at other times it will be impossible to say with any certainty whether or not ADHD is involved. On such occasions, focus directly on the behaviour, challenge or barrier in front of you – this is often the quickest route to a solution.

Parenting a child with ADHD and acting as his or her safe place, caregiver, advocate and more can be a very lonely and isolating task – so be sure to keep your support networks open. We learn so much from our peers, and while finding another parent experiencing the same sorts of challenges may not solve a given problem, just knowing that there is someone else in a similar position can provide a reassuring safety blanket. Other parents can teach us new things, expand our range of self-care options, and offer much-needed support – sometimes, asking for help is the bravest thing to do. We will look at parent support groups in more depth in Chapter 30.

How to help – be the world expert on your child

☞ Professionals will come and go in your own and your child's life – a teacher for a year, a SENCO for a school phase, a paediatrician or mental health professional for an indeterminate amount of time.

☞ As a parent, you are the one constant throughout the whole of your child's journey – you are the world expert on your child! You will remain so as they discover more about themselves throughout their lives, so learn as much as you can about them:

- Learn about what makes your child behave, respond and learn in the ways that they do.
- Understand the challenges your child faces and how best to support them.
- Identify your child's strengths and understand how to celebrate and channel them.
- Understand what may be around the corner as the inevitable challenges of adolescence and school transitions approach.

☞ Understand your child – better than anyone else in the world understands them. Be the world expert on your child!

Chapter 25: Before you know

Early identification and intervention is key to supporting children effectively as they grow up with ADHD and its challenges. As ADHD is a disorder of developmental delay, identifying indicators in infants and early childhood is not easy, and at present it is unusual for a child to be assessed or diagnosed prior to starting school. This is an area of current interest,

Key Point

As ADHD is a disorder of developmental delay, it is unusual for a child to be assessed prior to starting school.

however, and researchers have begun to make links between 'fussy' babies with poor sleep habits and a later diagnosis of ADHD. A study led by Mirja Helen Hemmi looked at excessive crying, issues with settled sleep and feeding challenges, and showed some links to 'persistent regulatory problems' in later childhood.[50] The risk was found to be higher for babies with challenges in several of these categories.

A range of behaviours displayed by normal babies could potentially be interpreted as indicators of ADHD – including excessive crying, poor attention span, restlessness and sudden outbursts. In most cases, there is no cause for concern – babies cry to express a need, they naturally have short attention spans and some babies are just difficult to settle to sleep. These early developmental behaviours should only be considered as risk factors for SEND when they persist beyond a point when other children of the same age are learning to regulate their needs and exercise more control.

When we spoke to William's mother, she recalled the early months with her eldest child as *"a relentless cycle of trying to get him to feed, then trying to get him to sleep, then trying to get him to stay asleep. Never happy, never settled and constantly uncomfortable. My friends described him as 'sensitive'; my sister, less kindly, called him 'high maintenance'."* Joe's mother told us that her son was diagnosed with colic, a condition associated with fussy babies, and Emily's mother Louise recalled that: *"From the age of three months Emily didn't sleep during the day for longer than twenty minutes. She had to be moving all the time or she would scream. I used to walk miles every day just to keep her on the move."*

Babyhood soon gives way to the toddler years, and this tends to be the stage at which parents begin to notice that their child may be different, or experience more challenges than other children. This may happen at

---

50 Hemmi M.H., Wolke, D., & Schneider, S. (2011). Associations between problems with crying, sleeping and/or feeding in infancy and long-term behavioural outcomes in childhood: a meta-analysis. *Archives of Disease in Childhood* 96: 622-9.

home or in early childcare and nursery settings. In all our parent case studies, the journey of identification began around ages three to four. Prior to Harry starting nursery, his mother Amy put his impulsivity down to being *"an active child and full of energy."* It was only when he started nursery that concerns were raised, with him *"getting easily frustrated with a task, and lashing out physically. He was always going from one activity to another and was very accident prone."* William's mother recalls having to leave a parent and toddler group because her son was pushing over children who were learning to stand and walk. She recalls being told by the group leader, *"Just ignore him, he's doing it for attention."* However, her embarrassment at the disapproving looks from the parents of his 'victims' led to her going home in tears.

A recent study looking more deeply into indicators of ADHD in toddlerhood found that formal assessments could be valid for children as young as two. More research is needed before firm conclusions can be reached but, as our case studies illustrate, it appears that the three key hallmarks of ADHD for children over three – inattention, hyperactivity and impulsivity – are often present in younger children. As with babies, it is important to distinguish between behaviours that may suggest a developmental disorder, and those behaviours that are normal for toddlers. The key question to consider is: "Is this behaviour developmentally appropriate for my child's age?" Belle's mother Faye told us that one of the first times she realised that her daughter was struggling was when Belle's younger sister reached the same ages and moved through them in a developmentally appropriate way. This prompted Faye to start asking herself questions; until then, she had simply put Belle's behaviour down to her being *"over sensitive and emotional and fussy."*

Sometimes patterns of behaviour are easier to spot with the benefit of hindsight. William's mother recalled bedtimes with wry humour: *"It was ridiculous looking back – we were trying to have a nice calm story like all the books say and he was hanging upside down off the bed, jumping on the pillows, snatching the book from my hands, thrusting another at me after one page, asking for a drink and talking about trains! Impulsive, hyperactive and no attention span – we should have known!"*

Joe's mother looked back with sadness as she recalled how, when she tried to put Joe to bed, her son would *"become physical towards me – this could be throwing toys, hitting, kicking and on occasion, trying to bite. Out of this whole journey, that was the hardest stage. I used to get so upset that I couldn't put my baby to bed without chaos ensuing."*

Matt's mother, Fiona, also recalled feelings of despair in Matt's early years. *"He was about three and Pickie the hamster was a much-loved pet. Matt would pet and feed her with no issues at all. Then one day, when he was* about three, Matt had been in the playroom with my friend's daughter and came out holding a very motionless Pickie on the flat surface of a badminton racquet. I was utterly distraught, and all Matt could say was that he 'wanted to see if she bounced'. I recall being in floods of tears on the phone to my mother declaring 'serial killers have to start somewhere'. Suffice to say no more hamsters were had for many years. This incident was probably also the first time I started to feel acutely embarrassed by my son's behaviour and feared the judgement of my peers. What sort of boy kills a hamster? What sort of parenting allows that to happen?"

How to help – toddler behaviour checklist

☞ A useful checklist to consider when observing your toddler's behaviour is as follows:

- Does he or she have consistent challenges with sitting still; is he or she constantly squirming, fidgeting and wiggling?
- Does he or she have difficulty holding attention on tasks, toys and games compared to children of a similar age?
- Does he or she consistently fail to listen and respond when spoken to directly?
- Does he or she get sidetracked easily, flitting from one activity to another or forgetting what he or she is doing?

☞ Dr. Mark Mahone of the Kennedy Krieger Institute in Baltimore recommends that parents of pre-school aged children also look for the following additional indicators of ADHD[51]:

- Dislikes or avoids activities that require paying attention for more than one or two minutes
- Talks a lot more and makes more noise than other children of the same age
- Climbs on things when instructed not to do so; gets into dangerous situations because of fearlessness
- Cannot hop on one foot by the age of four
- Frequently aggressive with playmates; has been removed from preschool/daycare for aggression

51 Kennedy Krieger Institute. (2021). Is it ADHD or Typical Toddler Behavior? Ten Early Signs of ADHD Risk in Preschool Age Children. Retrieved from https://www.kennedykrieger.org/stories/Is-it-adhd-or-typical-toddler-behavior-ten-early-signs-adhd-risk-preschool-age-children

So what next?

Noticing and understanding your child's behaviours as anything other than normal development can come as a shock. Feelings can be mixed; many parents we spoke with felt relief at finally being heard, and empowered that their child might soon have the support they needed. Once the ball started rolling, however, all our parents found it to be a lonely and scary time, with minimal direction and no clear avenue of support. Regrettably, luck of the draw is often a major factor at this stage. An overview of the assessment process was given in Chapter 3; it is worth noting that in the UK this pathway, though consistent in its expectations and outcomes, is wildly inconsistent in its specific route and can be something of a 'postcode lottery'.

For many children, starting primary school is when early identification of a neurodiverse need takes place. Following Harry's challenges in early years settings, his mother Amy suspected that something needed to be done but still put his hyperactivity down to an energetic child. She recalls that once he started school there were concerns about Harry's behaviour, with his teacher labelling him as emotionally immature and a distraction to others, and asking her whether she thought he was ready for school yet. This teacher had made the first steps in early identification of Harry's needs; what she failed to do was approach the issue with empathy, care or a solutions-based approach.

Sadly, this is a common experience; Matt's mother Fiona recalls raising concerns with his teacher when Matt was eight, and leaving *"with my fears utterly dismissed. I felt like many others before me – a useless, paranoid parent."* We have noted that children with ADHD hear 20,000 more negative messages by the age of ten than their neurotypical peers; regrettably, these negative messages can often also extend to their parents. How many 'difficult' children are simply not yet assessed or diagnosed, or haven't had their needs recognised for what they are – a neurological disability?

It is clear, then, that early identification of needs is critical to securing the help a child needs, and avoiding unhelpful and upsetting misunderstandings. But what does inattentive, impulsive and hyperactive behaviour look like in the classroom? The parents we spoke to had a range of early indicators that were observed when their children started school. These included:

- The child was finding school increasingly stressful.
- The school asked for hearing tests as the child was extremely loud.

- The child was struggling to make and uphold relationships in the playground, causing him or her a great deal of upset.
- The child appeared often to be in a 'dream world', not concentrating on classwork and falling behind with learning.
- There were complaints about the child not listening to the teachers, running off, swinging on chairs and touching or annoying classmates.
- The child would hurt other children when lost in play; e.g. one child bit a classmate believing he was a dinosaur at the time

For many parents we spoke to, the school SENCO was a reliable and supportive professional to support, organise and direct a referral for an ADHD assessment. Given that the process for parents can be a frustrating one, with lengthy waiting times, onerous forms and paperwork and a lack of communication from medical teams, a proactive SENCO can be a hugely helpful asset. When asked about the referral pathways they had experienced, our parents' responses all echoed similar themes:

- *"A frustrating journey. Thankfully his school has been super-supportive, which has definitely helped as we have heard next to nothing from the neurodevelopmental team he is under."*
- *"The journey to diagnosis has been a hard one. We reached out to a number of organisations including our GP, most of whom weren't helpful or forthcoming in terms of next steps required. In fact our GP seemed unwilling to make the referral as he felt that it would not get very far due to delays and lack of support in our system."*
- *"Thankfully the SENCO at his new school was extremely supportive and able to talk us through the process, make the referral and help us with the application."*
- *"I was happy with the school helping me as I had no idea who to turn to myself. I had lots of forms to fill in regarding her difficulties, and that sort of stuff is hard to put on paper."*

Sadly, for parents who are not lucky enough to have a supportive SENCO guiding them through the process, the wait of up to two years or more can be too long, and some seek a private assessment at their own cost in an effort to move forward with a treatment and support plan for their child.

H2h How to help – staying positive
How to Help **pre-diagnosis**

☞ **Fussy babies.** The early days, weeks and months with newborn infants can be an isolating time, and this can be exacerbated by a sleepless, fussy baby. Ensure that you access all the support available to you – midwives, health visitors, GP, Sure Start, and of course family and friends. If it all gets too much, ask for help!

☞ **Toddler frustrations.** All toddlers are testing; those with issues of hyperactivity, impulsivity and attention are exhaustingly so. Yet this is a critical time for development. Use positive techniques to teach and reinforce desired behaviours, and to avoid punishments or negative messages that may compound the child's difficulties.

☞ **Get a second opinion.** The first door that you open for support may not be the right one, and a second or even third opinion or pathway may be needed. This takes resilience and strength. Remember that you are the expert on your child, and if at first you don't get what you need, try again. Take a friend along to meetings for support.

☞ **Make a strong link in school.** Other than the home, your child's school or care setting will be where they spend the most time. Make a strong, trusting and supportive link with your child's SENCO, class teacher or another adult. Find someone who listens to you, understands your child and can support you both.

☞ **Keep notes.** The assessment process involves a lot of red tape. You will be asked many questions about your child, from pregnancy to the present day. Some parents find it useful to keep a notepad to write down challenges, observations or worries, and to draw on this when completing paperwork or attending appointments.

☞ **Keep forms.** If you have spent hours or days completing forms, make sure that you keep a copy before returning them – it is not unheard of for paperwork to go astray! In addition, make a clear note of the contact details for the teams that are looking after your child – names, phone numbers and email addresses.

Remember all the amazing things about your child.
Assessment focuses on challenges, barriers and concerns. It is
the nature of the process that the questions will feel negative,
and the form will feel like a permanent record of your child's
difficulties. You will not be asked how loving your child is, or
about their passions, interests, empathy, creativity, sports skills
or incredible zest for life. But remember all these things, and
keep them close to your heart.

Chapter 26: Let's have a good day

Day-to-day life with ADHD is not easy, and it can be exhausting. As we have seen, parenting a child with ADHD requires boundless energy and a huge amount of self care. Harry's mother Amy testifies to this – *"Harry needs attention, focus and support to get through the day"* – as does Joe's mother – *"Joe often seeks reassurance through the day, asks for hugs a lot, is super affectionate and playful – but loud!"* In this chapter, we will look at the day-to-day challenges that a parent of a child with ADHD may face, and work through some practical strategies to ensure that a good day is had by all!

Key Point

It is best to address only one challenge at a time, choosing the thing that is causing you the most difficulty at that particular moment.

Something to bear in mind throughout the course of each day is that it is nearly always best to address only one challenge at a time, choosing the thing that is causing you the most difficulty at that particular moment. It might feel that you have a wealth of challenges that you want or need to address, but trying to tackle getting ready for school, sibling rivalry, dinner time and bedtime all at once is likely to be overwhelming for you and your child. Try to choose one area to address and stick at it until it is better.

Structure and routine

Children with ADHD thrive on structure and routine, and having the same sequence of events and things to do each day is a vital part of helping them to manage. It is important that the routines and structures that you put in place are not just used as a short-term tactic, but embedded as a way of life that can have a long-term impact. Faye recalls her own experience: *"Belle needs routine – she needs to know where she is going and what she is doing. Some days are harder than others, but they aren't going away so it's a case of learning to deal with them."*

However hard we try to establish a structure to each day, life is not scripted and changes will sometimes happen. If you are aware of an approaching change to the normal routine, ensure that where possible you explain to your child what is coming and why. Forewarned is forearmed! If a change comes as a surprise and is out of your control, then be prepared for your child to find this difficult to manage. Matt's mother Fiona reflects on this: *"Heaven help us if we needed to change the plans. Extreme reactions."*

New and different things can cause upset for children with ADHD. Pre-warning helps to prepare children for what is going to happen, but you can also work together to plan for the change. For example, if you have an upcoming holiday to a new destination, spend a little time researching the place you are going and/or try an online walk-through. If your child is going on a school trip somewhere local that they haven't visited before, driving there on the previous weekend may help to lessen anxieties. Prepare carefully when taking your child to places that you know may cause stress or sensory overload; for example ear defenders may help in loud places, games in your bag will help with long waits, and many shopping centres, cinemas and theme parks have SEND-friendly events. It is always worth calling ahead to find out what adjustments can be made for people with specific needs.

Let's have a good morning

1. Be prepared

Managing the morning routine with a child who has attention and focus challenges requires preparation. Ensuring that everything is in its place and organised is a great starting point. Consider getting as much as possible ready the evening before, whether it's lunches in the fridge, uniform laid out on the floor or bags and shoes lined up at the door. To support your child in developing their executive functioning skills, involve them in these activities as much as possible. Where does your child put their school uniform when they take it off each day? Where do the school shoes live? Where should school bags hang? Involving your child in these thought processes means that when, inevitably, they ask "Where are my school shoes?" you can say "Where do we put the shoes when you come home from school?" instead of simply "In the shoe box." Some families have five drawers labelled Monday-Friday, and work with their children on a Sunday to pack them for with all that is needed the week ahead. This can support organisation and help your morning to run as smoothly as possible.

Visual timetables showing the order of the morning with images, symbols or photos can reassure children with ADHD and give them the feeling of security and predictability that they need. Having a checklist to work against will give them a sense of achievement too! Consider placement in an accessible location and how you will mark off each stage when it is completed – for example by ticking a picture, removing it from the chart or turning it over. Aim to wake your child at the same time each day and follow the same sequence of events – whatever works best for your family.

2. Getting dressed

Getting dressed can be difficult for children with ADHD, as it requires manual dexterity to deal with buttons and zips, working memory skills to know what to do in what order, organisation to find the required items, and the ability to stay on task and avoid distractions. For the last point, it would not be unusual to find a child with ADHD with one sock on, engrossed in playing with Lego because they have become distracted from dressing by the lure of their bedroom environment. In addition, for some children with ADHD, heightened sensory awareness can mean that some items of uniform cause physical discomfort – for example seams on socks, the reverse of an embroidered badge or the cuffs and collars of shirts.

H²h How to help – getting dressed

You can support your child with dressing in the following ways:

☞ **Help them to be organised.** Ensure that they have all they need and know where to find it. Label bedroom drawers with photographs, or have a large box that is prepared the night before with everything they need to get ready next day.

☞ **Have a step-by-step process to follow.** This could be a numbered list of items on the wall, or a visual model. Remember that children with ADHD have difficulties with working memory skills, so they will find it a challenge to follow a long list of steps without some reminding. This could be you verbally telling them each step, or a visual support to refer to independently in their room.

☞ **Set a time limit.** Giving your child a clear start and end time to the getting dressed process will support them in staying on task. Ask them to finish dressing before a favourite pop song finishes, use a timer on your phone or tablet and ask your child to choose the end tone/song, or use a visual device such as a sand timer.

☞ **Avoid distractions.** Where possible, try to have a limited number of distractions around – keep toys tidied away, and save tablets and other screens for their allocated portion of the day.

Support sensory needs. If your child is hypersensitive to the feel of their uniform, this can be supported by cutting out labels, washing new clothes before they are worn and/or wearing a base layer. Many uniform stockists are becoming more aware of the challenges faced by some children and are stocking uniform with minimal seams, soft waistbands and adjustments such as Velcro buttons. There are also online stockists of basic clothing items for children who are sensitive to touch – such as seamless socks!

3. Stay positive

As you decide on your family's morning routine, try to build in some positive mindset work to end the morning and support transition into the school day. This could be each family member saying one thing that they are grateful for today, or something that they're looking forward to in the day ahead. More broadly, try to keep all communications with your children as positive as possible. Slight tweaks can make a world of difference, so try the following:

- Tell them what you do want, not what you don't want.
- Follow an instruction with "thank you" before they have completed it.
- Praise the effort not the outcome – "I love how hard you tried to get dressed all by yourself!"
- Look for the good – catch your child doing the right thing, or trying to do the right thing, and praise it in the moment.

After school pick-up

When you collect your child from school, be mindful that the day has been much harder and more tiring for them than for their neurotypical classmates. They have had to work harder to remember instructions, manage emotions, meet behaviour expectations and avoid a classroom full of weird and wonderful distractions in order to settle to a task and do their work. This can cause a 'Coke bottle' effect of explosive meltdown. If you imagine that a stressful situation is like a bottle of Coke being shaken, and factor in the number of such situations faced by a child with ADHD during a typical school day, it should come as no surprise that when the day ends and the child comes face to face with their safe place – the trusted parent – the lid often pops off the bottle and the emotions explode out. Remember, this is actually a parenting win! When it all gets too much, your child explodes onto the person they love most and who loves them unconditionally – you.

How to help – the end of the school day

You can help your child through the end of the school day in several ways:

☞ Manage the transition. Be aware that your child will need some processing and adjustment time to move from school to home. Don't immediately bombard them with questions about their day; let them de-escalate and unwind slowly.

☞ Start a positive conversation. When your child is ready to talk, instead of asking if they had a good day which will lead to a closed yes/no answer, or asking what they did which is hard to remember, ask them to tell you something that made them smile, something that made them feel proud, something kind that somebody did, or something that was interesting. This slight change of tactic doesn't overload their recall skills, and it can start a pleasant conversation.

☞ Bring a snack. For children with ADHD, eating lunch surrounded by other people in a busy dinner hall can lead to a lot of stress and food going uneaten. Meeting them at the gate with something healthy to eat can help to prevent a hunger meltdown.

☞ Get moving! Your child may have had quite a static and still afternoon, especially as they move up through their school years. If you have time, stopping for a run in the park or a bounce on a trampoline can help to use up some much-needed energy.

Chapter 27: Let's have a good evening

Dinner time

Mealtimes can be a challenge for children with ADHD. They are required to focus attention, to deal with a range of sensory inputs (tastes, smells, noises) and to remember the social etiquette for a family meal – all at once! Some children also struggle with a limited palate. When we spoke to Joe's mother, she described how mealtimes could involve a range of challenges such as maintaining focus, introducing new foods that might cause gagging, and managing the time spent on the meal. They worked together as a family to improve this by minimising distractions, not overloading Joe's plate and offering lots of reassurance. You can make mealtimes an easier experience for your own family by considering some of the options set out below.

 How to help – dinner time

☞ **Plan ahead.** Structure and routine are important for children with ADHD, so create a weekly meal planner that allows your child to see what is coming on what day. This also helps with variety – the child may accept a day when the favourite food is not on the menu if he or she knows that tomorrow will be a different story!

☞ **Get them involved.** Involve your child as much as possible in meal planning. When children feel part of this process they can feel empowered as part of the family. Consider letting each family member choose one meal per week or per fortnight.

☞ **Guide the adventure.** Nominate one day a week as 'try something new day' – then choose and cook something together that your child has not tasted before. Research shows that it can take up to ten tries to decide if you like a new food or not,[52] so support your child in their taste adventures by explaining how their taste buds work, and that they are growing and changing as they get older. They might not be ready yet, but you could try again in future!

---

52 Loewen, R., & Pliner, P. (1999). Effects of prior exposure to palatable and unpalatable novel foods on children's willingness to taste other novel foods. *Appetite, 32*.

Dinner is served! Sitting still is likely to be a challenge for a child with ADHD. Only call them to the table when dinner is ready, to avoid waiting, and have a realistic expectation of how long they can sit at the table for. The ADHD Foundation suggest doubling the child's age as a rule of thumb, so a five year old might be able to sit still for ten minutes and a ten year old for twenty minutes.

 Find the best approach. For many children food on a plate works best – there is a clear expectation of what they must eat, it is not overwhelming and they know that they like it. Other families find that a buffet approach helps expose their children to new foods, textures and tastes without the pressure of it being on the plate.

 Minimise distractions. Turn off the TV and radio, and avoid lots of coming and going at mealtimes. Your child may become easily bored at the dinner table, so involve them in family conversation and engage with their interests. Ask them to tell you about a favourite video game, or a game they played with their friends.

Bedtime

Just as ADHD isn't something that children grow out of, it doesn't vanish at bedtime. The busy mind of a child with ADHD can often continue racing well into the night and be almost impossible to switch off. Needless to say, this is not conducive to restful sleep. Research shows that children and young people with ADHD are more likely to suffer with sleep disorders, including getting to sleep and staying asleep.[53] Lack of sleep can affect mood and cause mental fatigue, which can then exacerbate the challenges that children with ADHD already face with attention and managing impulsive behaviours.

Expert View

"Disturbances of sleep in people with ADHD are common, but are almost completely ignored by our current diagnostic system and ADHD research."

William Dodson

Psychiatrist William Dodson has stated that prior to puberty, ten to fifteen percent of children with ADHD have trouble getting to sleep – double the number of neurotypical children who experience such difficulties. Sadly, the picture does not improve over time: half of all children with ADHD have difficulty falling asleep almost every night by their early

---

53 Pachecho, D. (2021) *ADHD and Sleep*. Sleep Foundation.

teenage years, and more than seventy percent of adults with ADHD report regularly spending more than one hour trying to fall asleep at night.[54]

It is also worth noting that even when a child or young person manages to get to sleep, this can be restless. Sleep research studies have shown that children with ADHD tend to move more during the night.[55] Deep sleep is one of the four sleep cycles that we all go through – it is the opportunity for our brain to create and store our memories, and a chance to organise our thoughts ready for the next day. It also allows the brain some much needed rest. In Chapter 21 we saw that children of different ages require differing amounts of sleep – this table is shown again below:[41]

- Infants 4 to 12 months: 12-16 hours of sleep, including naps
- Children 1 to 2 years: 11-14 hours of sleep, including naps
- Children 3 to 5 years: 10-13 hours of sleep, including naps
- Children 6 to 12 years: 9-12 hours of sleep
- Teenagers 13 to 18 years: 8-10 hours of sleep

With this in mind, supporting a child with ADHD to practise good sleep hygiene and maximise their healthy sleep will not only make life easier for them during the night; it will make their days more manageable, too.

---

54 Dodson, W. (2021) *ADHD and Sleep Problems: This is Why You're Always So Tired.* ADDitude
55 Wajszilber D. et al. (2018). Sleep disorders in patients with ADHD; Impact and Management challenges. *Nature and Science of Sleep* 10: 453-480.

How to help – sleeping

☞ **Routine.** That magic word again. Children with ADHD need a clear routine to wind down, transition from evening to bedtime and prepare for a good night's sleep. Beds and sleep do not appeal to children with ADHD, so plenty of warning to stop the activity they are doing will help. Keeping a set bedtime also supports the brain and internal body clock in becoming familiar with the routine.

☞ **Establish a bedtime.** To find out the ideal bedtime, work backwards using what you know about how much sleep your child needs and when they need to get up in order to be ready to start the day. Here is your bedtime goal! It is best to try to also keep to the same routine at weekends and during holidays.

☞ **Allow winding down time.** Set a routine that works for you and your family. It could include some of the following elements:

- **A warm bath.** Warm water can help regulate the body's temperature and prepare for a state of sleep.

- **Time to talk.** The brain of a child with ADHD is hard to slow down – allocate 'talk time' in order to give your child a safe place to empty their mind of some of its racing thoughts. You could discuss something positive that happened during the day, or something exciting that is happening tomorrow.

- **Thoughts journal.** The things you discuss during talk time, or any broader worries or concerns, can be noted down in a journal, which is completed together then put away. This provides a visual support to the child that the issue has left the bedroom, and will not disturb their sleep.

- **Bedtime story.** We are never too old for a bedtime story! It is an opportunity to end the evening by sharing a favourite tale, or to capture a child's attention with new adventures. Helping your child with a book they cannot yet read alone supports brain development and language acquisition skills.

- **Leave some noise.** Lying alone in a room with only a busy mind for company can spell disaster for a child with ADHD. You can help with this by playing an audio book, podcast, sleep meditation or even just 'white noise'. Keeping the sensory input steady can help to calm the brain.

☞ **Sleep environment.** Try to keep the sleep space cool, dark and clutter free. Aim to have your child off screens an hour before bedtime, as blue light can impact their circadian rhythms. Keep lighting levels low and warm using dimmer switches or lamps.

☞ **Bed covers.** For children with ADHD who move more than others at night time, the bed covers can end up in a serious tangle. You could try using a weighted blanket, compression blankets or a double duvet on a single bed so that it can be tucked under the mattress. Some children with ADHD prefer to use a sleeping bag. All of these options give children the sensory input they may be craving, and support them to manage their restlessness.

Chapter 28: Two parent and child journeys in their own words

For the parents of a child with ADHD, learning about the condition and the likely road ahead can be a daunting and uncertain experience. Parents often say that they knew early on that their child was somehow 'different', but they didn't understand why or what it would mean in terms of the short- and long-term impact on their child and their family. Because ADHD is so often a journey into the unknown, hearing from parents who have already taken it – and how they have sought to help their children with ADHD – can be a hugely important form of support. In this chapter, we will hear more about Harry and Emily from the perspective of their mothers, Amy and Louise.

> ## Key Point
>
> *Because ADHD is often a journey into the unknown, hearing from parents who have already taken it can be a hugely important form of support.*

Amy: *"Harry has always been an active child and full of energy, but I began to notice that he was different to others his age when he was about three. Although he was hyperactive, I had always put that down to him being a toddler with lots of energy. When he started nursery other traits started to show in his behaviour, such as getting easily frustrated with a task and lashing out physically, or a lack of imagination or interest in role playing.*

"He was always going from one activity to the next and was very accident prone, always falling off play equipment, running into tables and so on. The only thing he would ever pay any attention to and focus on was trains – watching trains on YouTube and building train sets. When he started school, he struggled to settle and after a few biting incidents and concerns over him distracting others in his class I was called in to have a meeting.

"Initially Harry's teachers labelled him as emotionally immature and a distraction for others, and they challenged me as to whether he was ready for school yet. With hindsight I think that this primary school in rural Somerset was not ready to handle a child with Harry's needs. Regardless, it was very hard for me to hear that the teachers had concerns over Harry's behaviour; it felt like confirmation that something was different about him."

When parents become concerned that something is 'different' about their child, they seek support – and this typically leads to a process of assessment and possible diagnosis. However, the journey is often a far from easy one.

Amy: *"The journey to Harry's diagnosis has been hard. We moved from Somerset to Kent when he was in Year 3, and a combination of a new environment and a change of routine made it clear to his teachers and our family that Harry was likely to have a cognitive or behavioural disorder of some kind. On the one hand this was easy to accept as I had always known that he was different – he seemed to be permanently running on a motor with boundless energy, and he was often difficult to control in comparison to other children. But on the other hand, it was difficult to acknowledge that he really did have special needs, and that we required support to help him.*

"We decided to go down the path of seeking a formal diagnosis. We reached out to a number of organisations, including our GP. Most of them weren't particularly helpful or forthcoming in terms of the steps required; in fact our GP seemed unwilling to make a referral as he felt that it would not get far due to delays and lack of support in the system. Thankfully the SENCO at Harry's new school was extremely supportive and able to talk us through the process, make the referral and help us with the paperwork.

"We made a formal application to seek a diagnosis of ADHD through the NHS. Whilst completing all the appropriate forms we waited over a year for an assessment date and appointment. In the meantime Harry's behaviour continued to deteriorate. In Year 5, with his education suffering a further significant impact from the COVID-19 pandemic, we decided that we could not afford to wait any longer and we paid privately to have him assessed."

There is no doubt that, for parents of children who show traits consistent with ADHD, working closely with the school can have major advantages.

Louise: *"Emily's anxiety levels had been building over the year prior to starting school; during Year 1 they became extreme, and she began to describe her head as 'going crazy'. She would be in tears each morning, saying: 'I just can't concentrate at school' and 'why is my brain going crazy?' I had to hand her over at the school gate screaming and distressed every day. I remember her saying: 'sometimes I just go into my head and get trapped'. To hear your five-year-old say these things is heartbreaking.*

"I decided to start the next school year by talking to the class teacher and suggesting to her that Emily seemed to have some issues with attention. To my relief it seemed that she had already noticed, and I thought that

maybe we would get some help. She said that Emily struggled to start on an activity and get organised. The teacher would have to go to her and say: 'What do you need? You need a pencil; do you have one?' and prompt her on every step. The teacher also had to stand by Emily while she got changed for PE to prompt her throughout, because she would get distracted so easily.

"At this point I started to read up on ADHD, and I decided to attend a conference. I sat and held back the tears all day. They were describing my daughter. It was the first time I had been in a room full of people who understood her. I had another meeting with the teacher, in which I told her that I felt that Emily might have ADHD and that we had decided to have her assessed. The teacher's response was 'Oh I don't think so, I've had other children with ADHD and she's not like them.' Instead of being supported, Emily began to come home from school saying that she had been told she was lazy and didn't try hard enough. She was six years old.

"We went ahead with the assessment, and at the age of six and a half Emily was diagnosed with moderate combined type ADHD. We decided to start medication a couple of months later, and it made a huge difference to her quality of life. We noticed from day one that the medication enabled her to do things that she had never been able to do before. Her brother asked her to play a board game with him. They sat down and played it and she followed the whole game without having to be reminded every time that it was her turn, where the dice was and where her piece was. Her brother even accused her of cheating at one point; I braced myself for the inevitable meltdown but instead she just explained, calmly, why she hadn't cheated."

Emily's story raises the issue of considering medication to support children with ADHD with learning, behaviour and socialisation issues. Strict protocols are in place with regards to the option of prescribing medication. The UK National Institute for Health and Care Excellence (NICE) guidelines include a comprehensive section on medication to treat ADHD symptoms, and emphasise the importance of patients having a full baseline assessment incorporating social circumstances, mental health and physical health before starting any medication. The guidance differentiates between immediate and modified release preparations, and specifies a trial period of six weeks. It also advises that once treatment dose has been stabilised, prescribing and monitoring of ADHD medication should be carried out under Shared Care Protocol/Arrangements with primary care physicians.[56]

56 Hospital Pharmacy Europe. (2020) *Diagnosis and Management of ADHD: Summary of NICE guidance.* Published 18th August 2020.

The stigma of considering medication to support children with ADHD has lessened over recent years, but nevertheless this is still a huge step for any family to take. A deluge of negative media coverage has led to those who choose medication for their child being judged unfairly, and to many people viewing the use of medication as a form of 'chemical cosh' used to quieten children. In fact this is wholly incorrect; ADHD is a neurobiological issue, and as such it may require neurobiological support. Despite this, medication remains a divisive issue among families, friends and even some teachers.

The number of medication options licensed for supporting children for ADHD has increased over time; however, doctors will usually suggest an initial trial of more established products such as stimulants. For parents and their children, a trial is always necessary to weigh advantages against any disadvantages in terms of any potential side effects or other factors.

Amy: *"We were advised to try Harry on methylphenidate to help manage his behaviour, and we are currently working through the best dose and combination of medicine. We remain in the early stages of this, and while we have seen improvements – notably with regards to his attention span and his understanding of his own emotions – we have also had some unforeseen consequences. We have been able to see more autistic behaviours come to the fore that we are sure have always been there but were previously masked and hidden by his ADHD. This has been tough for all of us and for Harry in particular. It almost feels like, for the first time in his life, his medication has allowed him time to reflect on confusing thoughts and feelings that, whilst they are not new, appear so and have created a broader set of issues for him to manage."*

Medication, however, is only one option for supporting children with ADHD – albeit it often proves a very effective one. Many parents continue to live day-to-day with children who may be unpredictable in terms of their impulsive behaviour, and this can put them under tremendous strain.

Louise: *"I had an unexpected phone call from the school head teacher last year to tell me that Emily had scaled an eight foot fence whilst watching a demonstration by another class during a PE lesson, and she wondered what Emily had been thinking. In explaining that it was possibly just an impulse, and as such there was probably not much prior thought process, I told her that I had lost count of the number of times Emily had climbed on top of our car as quick as a flash and used the windscreen as a slide!*

"We have learned to pre-empt possible triggers and to avoid or distract from certain situations, but also to pick our battles and to use language to

help Emily stop, think about her behaviours and make choices herself. Of course, it's not appropriate for Emily to be standing on our car roof – but a cry of 'No stop!' will fall on deaf ears, whereas a calm (as calm as you can be when your child is on top of your car...) 'Emily, why should you not stand up there?' will usually make her stop, think about the dangers and climb down herself."

One crucial area in terms of supporting the parents of children with ADHD is to recognise the value of support groups – something we will return to in Chapter 30. Knowing that you are not alone, or that you will not be judged by others going through similar experiences, can be absolutely vital for building self-esteem and resilience among all members of the family.

Amy: *"As parents we are often exhausted, disappointed and frustrated all in one breath. Some days are easier than others, but on a bad day we can feel particularly useless, embarrassed, sad and angry for the challenges that Harry has to go through. Luckily, with the exception of his new-born sister, his siblings are older and more socially mature. They accept and manage him as best they can, but obviously his ADHD puts a significant strain on our family life."*

Although life with ADHD can undoubtedly be challenging, when the correct mechanisms are in place and people are able to work together in proactive, positive ways, children with ADHD can and will achieve successful outcomes.

Louise: *"With the adaptations in place and proper understanding of her needs, Emily is doing amazingly at school. She is now in Year 5 and is able to spend the whole day in the classroom. She still gets distracted, zones out at times, cannot complete great volumes of written work and has a TA to help her when she needs it, but she is gaining independence and learning to understand and manage her ADHD more and more."*

Looking at the reality of living with ADHD from the child's perspective is also important if we are to successfully help both families and schools.

Amy: *"Harry was asked what he liked about having ADHD. He said that he likes the fact that he has lots of energy; he thinks this makes him better at sports which makes him happy. He doesn't like it that he fidgets, or that he says and does things that get him into trouble. He doesn't like being shouted at, and he said that less shouting would help him to like having ADHD more.*

"While Harry is happy with his diagnosis and finds it helpful to understand that he is different, we know that he has some challenges which also require management and support. The constant strain to try and be good puts a lot of pressure on him. This is partly pressure he puts on himself to try and get rewards – or just to get through the day without negative consequences – but also pressure that we put on him. Family, school and societal norms can be extremely stressful and sometimes all-consuming for Harry. Sometimes it gets too much, and without realising it he instantly becomes frustrated and aggressive without realising what caused his stress or upset in the first place.

"We would like Harry to better understand his own brain, his ADHD and how this impacts him in different environments, and to help him become more socially mature and self-aware. Also we want him to understand that he isn't just ADHD – there's lots more to him, including struggles and emotions that are faced by all kids his age. It would be great if there was a forum or safe space where kids could talk to each other about how their emotions relate to everyday life, to help Harry recognise these better in himself and others."

This raises a critical point about why everybody in a school community should be involved with understanding ADHD – including the pupils. We advocate that all students in a school community should be taught about neurodiversity in the same way that other forms of diversity are discussed as part of a planned and structured whole school programme. When the challenges associated with ADHD are 'out in the open' and understood by all, it becomes much easier for those who face those challenges to cope.

Ultimately, no matter what other forms of support are in place, it will often be down to the parents to be the rock on which their child totally depends to support and advocate for them when times get tough, uncertain and stressful. Parents may be worried – not just about short-term situations, but about the longer-term future – and joining a local or national support group is strongly advised. Here, parents will meet others who will face the same concerns and challenges – but who also have the same hopes and dreams.

We will leave the last word to Emily's mother:

Louise: *"While we know that there will be more challenges to face, Emily's excitement and enthusiasm for life is infectious – and there's never a dull moment with our beautiful, cleaver, funny, crazy, unique girl!"*

How to help – the parent and child journey of ADHD

☞ **Trust your instincts.** Parents often need to battle on behalf of their children to get recognition and support – especially when family or even professionals say that a young child will "grow out of it." If your instincts tell you that something isn't right, trust them.

☞ **Persevere.** Assessment and diagnosis procedures can be complex, time-consuming and frustrating. However difficult things seem to be, it is worth persevering as you will have more support options with an accurate assessment. If the NHS pathway isn't working for you, taking a private route may be worth the short-term outlay.

☞ **Collaborate.** Working closely with your child's school is vital to supporting them academically, socially and through assessment. Every child needs a champion within school and parents need to identify which member of staff will take on that role if the obvious candidates do not appear to be 'stepping up'.

☞ **Be open minded.** Medication plays an important role in supporting many children with ADHD with issues of learning, behaviour and socialisation. Parents should be aware of the range of available ADHD medications, understand the benefits and side effects of each type, and act as partners to monitor the effects of dosages on their child's ADHD symptoms and general health and wellbeing.

☞ **Walk a mile in their shoes.** It's a good idea to ask children how they themselves feel about having ADHD, in order to help them make sense of their experience and also for their peers to better understand their behaviours. This should take place in a sensitive and structured way, perhaps as part of PHSE lessons.

☞ **Team up.** Parents of children with ADHD should try to join a parent ADHD support group, in order to learn from the experiences of others and to sustain themselves for the journey ahead.

Chapter 29: ADHD in the teenage years

The American author Mark Twain famously said: "When I was a boy of 14, my father was so ignorant I could hardly stand to have the old man around. But when I got to be 21, I was astonished at how much he had learned in seven years." If Twain's witticism conveys how confusing and hard to navigate the world is for the average teenager, then what must the challenges be like for a teenager with the developmental differences of ADHD, or for the parents and teachers who seek to support them?

ADHD is most often diagnosed in primary school, partly because it is relatively easy to spot in hyperactive boys. However, if a child has inattentive-type ADHD (perhaps quietly staring out of a window or leaving work undone), then signs may be missed during this time. This can often be the case with girls, but it is also true of some boys. Studies show that up to 85% of children with ADHD continue to experience symptoms into their adolescent years, and that 60% of them become adults with ADHD. The impact of symptoms may increase or decrease over time depending on the individual's brain development and the specific challenges they face in school or at work.

By the teenage years, the symptoms of ADHD plus any co-existing conditions are likely to mean that most teenagers with ADHD will experience higher levels of some or all of the following issues relative to peers of the same age:

- Distractibility, boredom and lack of focus
- Disorganisation and forgetfulness over basic issues
- Hyperactivity, fidgeting and restlessness
- Heightened emotionality and frustration
- Impulsivity and poor decision making
- Poor concentration and trouble finishing tasks

Ironically, some teenagers with ADHD do have a few specific activities or tasks with which they have no difficulty, and with which they may indeed thrive. Examples might include sports, video games, art, music or a range of other practical activities. This can be a source of confusion, as in such cases parents may wrongly assume that their teenagers are simply choosing to make an effort when it suits them. The reality is that when individuals with ADHD are able to sustain an interest in and focus on what they are doing, they can be extremely productive and successful.

Many teenage issues encountered at home, at school, and in social settings arise due to neurological developmental delays. It is believed that ADHD is connected to weak executive functioning skills – that is, skills that help us with regulating behaviour, setting goals, balancing responsibilities and learning to function independently. Problems with executive functioning can also affect a number of other skills that are critical to school and life success:

- Response inhibition (being able to stop an action if a situation suddenly changes)
- Working memory
- Emotional control
- Flexibility
- Sustained attention
- Task initiation
- Planning and organisation
- Time management
- Goal-directed persistence (sticking with a task when it becomes 'boring' or difficult)
- Metacognition (awareness and understanding of one's own thought processes)

On average, these executive skills don't fully develop for most individuals until their early twenties. For individuals with ADHD, it can be three to five years later. As a result of this developmental delay, teenagers with ADHD may unfairly be labelled as 'lazy' or 'oppositional' because their behaviour does not match that of their neurotypical peers. They can also lag behind in emotional maturity. Experts believe that, due to developmental delays, a young person with ADHD may not achieve the emotional maturity of a neurotypical 21-year-old until they reach their mid or even late thirties.

Most well-adjusted teenagers will struggle with peer pressure, academic expectations, and emotional and physical changes during adolescence. However, teenagers with ADHD face an extra set of challenges. Higher expectations and a drive for independence can often trigger impulsivity traits, just at a time when they may be facing transitional milestones such as encountering alcohol and forming relationships with new or different friends.

For parents trying to navigate these challenges, working closely with the school and finding a specialist or counsellor who is experienced in working with teenagers with ADHD will be vital. With a combination of practical behaviour advice, structured but flexible family and home management, and open-minded consideration of medication options, parents can successfully support their teenagers to avoid or minimise risks for negative outcomes.

The accounts below from two of our mothers, Sheila and Fiona, regarding their sons' experiences at secondary school during their teenage years, illustrate some of the pressures and challenges of these times.

Sheila: *"Secondary school was a better prospect for Martin; he had a brilliant SENCO who really 'got' him, and he made a small circle of friends who he stuck with throughout his secondary school years. He was never going to be a great achiever, but he got some good results."*

Fiona: *"All through secondary school Matt was a model pupil. Each year he received a prize because his Effort scores were among the highest in his year group. The year he left he was awarded a special prize for all-round achievement. He left with a raft of decent GCSEs, including a couple of A's.*

"I did have to support him along the way as Matt learns a little differently, and the way knowledge was tested in GCSEs often didn't suit him. He had a flair for language (his teacher said "he sees patterns no one else sees" – you don't say!), so he took his French exam early. This was fine as I was quite good at French at school, so I was happy to coach and prepare him in the way he needed. Then, because he passed French, he was chosen to do Spanish. I didn't know any Spanish but his expectation was for me to do the same as I had done for French, so guess who started to learn Spanish too! I regret my coaching abilities fell very short where it came to Maths, which I find impenetrable, so a very patient tutor was employed!

It was not all plain sailing, however. Although both these young men found supportive schools through the efforts of their parents, a common struggle for teenagers with ADHD is the issue of socialisation – along with issues of bullying by peers and sometimes also by members of staff.

Fiona: *"However, Matt was bullied. The usual stuff of name calling, throwing things at him in class and having his pants pulled down in PE. However the aspect of this that really affected him was being shunned. No one would talk to him. He spent lunchtimes and breaks in the library, keeping out of the way.*

"Supporting Matt through this was so challenging. The school were as supportive as they could be – I had no complaints with the way they handled the situation. I gave him some techniques to help deal with the bullies, but my overriding advice was that he 'just had to get through these few years'. I don't think I've ever felt so impotent. I'd see him off to school knowing he was in for yet another tough day. I was so very proud of him as he just put his head down and got on with it. He wanted to go on the school trip to France. I waited with him, watching all the other kids arrive and pair off into their little groups, and then I had to watch Matt walk onto the coach on his own and sit down alone. My heart broke. He was such a brave lad.

"In Year 9 Matt was referred to the Special Needs lunchtime club. Oh my goodness what a breakthrough! He loved the games, playing football and simply being away from everyone else. His life at school was so much happier from then on."

Meanwhile for Martin...

Sheila: *"Secondary school, the RE teacher tearing his work up in front of him and the whole class – not once but three times – then isolating him at the back of the classroom with empty desks either side of him. Writing in his journal: 'does not listen, can't concentrate'. Time for Mummy to have a word..."*

For both boys there is no doubt that the teenage years were a real struggle; however, a common factor in their overcoming adversity was having determined parents who were ready to support their child come what may.

Taking a strengths-based perspective

An area of research that is rapidly growing in importance focuses on the idea that ADHD provides individuals not just with difficulties, but also with also strengths – and that if this perspective is nurtured through the teenage years, then it can promote successful outcomes. A recent study identified personality strengths associated with ADHD as shown below:[57]

- **Energetic:** Some individuals with ADHD often have seemingly endless amounts of energy, which they are able to channel toward success on the playing field, in school or at work.

---

57 Boot, N., Nevicka, B., & Baas, M. (2017) Subclinical symptoms of attention-deficit/ hyperactivity disorder (ADHD) are associated with specific creative processes. *Personality and Individual Differences*, 114/1: 73-81

- **Spontaneous:** Some people with ADHD can turn impulsivity into spontaneity. They may be the life and soul of the party, or they may be more willing to try new things and break free from the status quo.

- **Creative and inventive:** ADHD may give a person a different perspective on life, and encourage them to approach situations and tasks with a thoughtful eye. As a result, some people with ADHD may be inventive thinkers – or generally original, artistic and creative.

- **Hyper focused:** Some people with ADHD become hyper focused – so intently focused on a task that they do not even notice the world around them. The benefit of this is that when given an assignment, they may be able to complete it without breaking concentration.

By focusing on the positive personality strengths of teenagers with ADHD rather than the challenges they face, this study was able to point to the following personal qualities that many of them also share:

- Ability to find unique solutions to difficult problems.
- Adventurous, courageous, thinks 'outside the box'.
- Ability to discern patterns where others see chaos.
- Ability to talk about many different topics at one time.
- Constant evolution, continual learning.
- Good in a crisis – some of the most stressful jobs are staffed by people with ADHD.
- Seemingly endless desire to try new ideas, tasks and projects.
- Empathetic and intuitive.
- Entrepreneurial.
- Continual source of new ideas, methods and strategies.
- Ability to see many if not all sides of a situation.

Therefore, although ADHD traits may well pose significant challenges for learning, behaviour and socialisation, for those individuals who are willing and able to adapt they can also offer a platform to develop areas of strength towards future opportunities. This certainly proved to be the case for Matt and Martin. As we have seen they both struggled at school; at the time of writing, Matt is a Ford Prototype Mechanic and Martin is a Police Officer.

H2h How to help – ADHD in the teenage years

☞ You must take care of yourself to take care of them. The teenage years can be difficult for all parents, but for children with ADHD the challenges can be immense, and patience can be difficult.

☞ Try to keep a log of all the assessments, supports and positive approaches taken by one school or year group to share with the next. Make sure that communication with relevant Heads of Year, SENCOs or learning support departments are constant.

☞ Know that sometimes 'the village raises the child' – and if they aren't prepared to certain information from you, they may take it from another family member or close friend. Don't take this personally; it's not about you, it's about them.

☞ If your teenager is on medication, ensure you have regular reviews with health care professionals to monitor dosage and side effects. Some teenagers will resist taking medication and obviously you cannot force this; however what you can do is suggest they take responsibility for their choices on the issue. Sometimes a school counsellor or equivalent can be more effective in this area.

☞ Socialisation issues and peer relationships can be very difficult, and you can't really involve yourself in this area unless of course you find out that your child is being bullied. If this is the case, then you should contact the school – or relevant agencies if it is outside school. Joining clubs or societies where there is a spread of ages can work well, as teenagers with ADHD tend to get on better with people who are younger or older than themselves.

☞ Consider ADHD's strengths as well as its challenges. Understand that ADHD can provide some advantages in terms of seeing the world differently and adapting to it, and that potential employers for example may welcome these differences in the workplace.

Chapter 30: You are not alone

It is often said that a problem shared is a problem halved. For families living with children with ADHD, the impact can often be overwhelming – and as a result parents can feel very isolated and alone. Concerns at school are usually addressed by the SENCO or the wider school SEND department, but options to support families at home can be difficult to find and access. In such circumstances, talking to other parents and sharing experiences with them can be an absolute lifeline – and potentially invaluable in terms of finding out what additional forms of support are available locally.

Key Point

Talking to other parents can be a lifeline – and potentially invaluable in terms of finding out what additional forms of support are available locally.

The story of Addup, as told by its founder

"Addup stands for 'Attention Deficit Disorders: Uniting Parents'. The organisation started life in 1996, when a group of local Essex parents whose children had all been recently diagnosed with ADHD were brought together by Dr Kanagasabai Puvanendran, or 'Dr Puva', as he was affectionately known, to support each other. At that time ADHD was a new diagnosis. I had never heard of it until my son was diagnosed, and it seemed no one in our area had heard of it either!

"We began to organise coffee mornings and invited guests along for advice on starting our group. Andrea Bilbow from ADDISS (the national Attention Deficit Disorder Information and Support Service) was one, and the manager of PACT (Parents of Autistic Children Together) was another. After a while Dr Puva organised a get together with Havering, Barking and Dagenham parents for us to become more formal. That night I put my hand up; exactly what for, I was unsure, but I wanted to help my boys and this was a way to do it!

"We met on a regular basis and decided on roles and responsibilities. I was given the role of taking enquiries, which I did – and listened to so many stories similar to my own. There were so many issues – mostly related to school, children being excluded and a lack of understanding amongst staff. At the time this was understandable, as we were all still learning about ADHD.

"Dr Puva gave us £500 and a library of books to start, and with help we developed a Constitution and registered as a Charity in 1997. We wanted to raise awareness of ADHD, and for professionals to meet with us and take us seriously. That was hard. We felt we were seen as a group of interfering parents that wanted to make a fuss. The media at the time was very unkind; there was so much negativity about ADHD, with headlines like 'is it real or just an excuse for bad parenting?', 'parents drug their children for a quiet life', and my favourite, 'the Ritalin cosh'. This put even more pressure on parents of children with ADHD to ask themselves: 'am I doing the right thing?'

"I even questioned myself; I knew that the medication was making a massive difference to my son and to our family, but I felt that parents' confidence to even get a referral was being reduced because of the stigma attached and the idea of other people knowing 'there is something wrong with my child.' However, children were struggling in the classroom, exclusions were rising and families were breaking down. The media portrayed the typical family with ADHD as living on benefits in a tower block, with children by different fathers and a burnt-out car on the road outside. In fact families with ADHD come from all backgrounds; we owned our house, my husband worked and we had holidays. But the media didn't want to see that side.

"We needed to change perceptions and raise awareness of ADHD and its positive aspects, but a formal referral process didn't really exist at that time. It was hit and miss as to whether you got referred at all, and you usually started with your GP who had little or no knowledge of ADHD and didn't know where to send the child, (this hasn't changed much!). So we started to bang on doors, and we wouldn't go away so they had no choice but to talk to us. Eventually they listened and agreed to cooperate with us, and working with Health, Education and Social Services in Havering, Barking and Dagenham we helped to produce a Protocol for the Identification and Management of ADHD. This took four years as changes in staff caused delays, but the finished product launched in 2001 and although the process has changed over time the same format is still used. It worked then, and it works now.

"Sadly, knowledge of how to manage ADHD is still not out there. It is only groups like ours that work directly with families, and we are very few. Many similar groups were started around the same time as Addup, but most folded as they didn't get support from their services and funding was hard to find. Who wants to fund 'naughty children' as ours became known?

"After the Protocol was launched, we needed to decide what was next for Addup. Havering opened a new CVS (Council for Voluntary Service – a place where local community organisations can speak to each other and cooperate), so we went along to a meeting to find out more and get our name out there. Once again, I put my hand up! I was now on the Committee for the new CVS; this was daunting, but it proved to be a godsend. Kim, the CEO, took us under her wing – she helped me with funding applications, and I learned so much from being on this Committee. It led to training for my own Committee, and in 2002 with a successful bid assisted by Kim we offered our first summer of activities for children with ADHD and their siblings. It ran for three weeks, three days a week, and we had thirty-five children attend. Now we run for four weeks, five days a week, and we have to allocate places as we have more than seventy young people participating.

"That first summer project was a great starting point for us – we had learned so much about the children that we began to develop activities that could meet their needs and the needs of their parents. By this time, most of the original Addup committee had left or moved on. I stayed and began to take on the role of Manager. As a parent who left school with no qualifications there was lot to learn. I was fortunate to be sponsored by Kim to complete an NVQ level 4 in Business Management, and although I know you can't fail an NVQ I was very proud of myself when I got the certificate to say I had passed!

"I had also applied for funding to open a Centre. The bid was successful, and the Addup Drop-in Centre became our new home. I finally moved out of the cupboard under the stairs. We started to deliver more activities, family days out and Christmas parties, and all the while we were learning. Learning how to run a charity, learning how to manage staff and volunteers, learning about health and safety and child protection law – the list was endless. With the funding we were able to employ someone to manage our finances, and after seven years as a volunteer we also finally got funding for my post. I had to apply and be interviewed, but I got the job.

"Addup went from strength to strength: we were providing school holiday and after school clubs, along with support in schools and other settings, help with forms and other red tape, and just a listening ear, a cup of coffee and a tissue when needed. Members numbers continued to increase, and soon we were averaging about 150 families a year on our membership. Some Addup families stay forever, some for just a couple of years; whenever they choose to leave, we hope that we have helped them on their way. Some families return later when new concerns raise their head – our door is always open.

"There were some very hard times, when funding started to dry up. I applied to many sources, but it seems that ADHD is not a 'popular' thing to fund. Getting salaried posts funded was hardest of all, and there came a point when I was handed my redundancy notice. I was devastated, but not out just yet. That year, 2009, we were named Best Community Group at the Havering Business Awards organised by the Local Authority and business community, so we campaigned and with straight backs and heads we approached the Local Authority and asked for money. Parents had confirmed a need for Addup, and the Authority had just given us an award for our work, so I asked: 'How much will a child with ADHD cost you to deal with if we aren't here?' It did the trick – we got the money and Addup survived. This gave us the breathing space we needed to build our reserves and seek other funding.

"As expected, the statutory funding ceased three years later. We had learned not to be reliant on it as we knew it wouldn't last; we had sourced other funding and instigated fundraising activities to keep our heads above the parapet. This has always been the hardest part of my job – being responsible for bringing in money to keep us going. We have been to the edge many times and it has caused me many sleepless nights. But we had started to see the fruits of our early work with young adults going to university and succeeding in their chosen paths, families relying on us for support, and new faces coming through our door who deserved the same life chances as any other child. Addup needs to be there for all of them, so we fight on.

"Like the Dickens character Mr Micawber, we are always optimistic that 'something will turn up.' We have to believe this to survive; there have been many times when we could have thrown in the towel, but then one of our children would shine and we would know that we needed to carry on, sleepless nights or not, so as not to let them down. Two years ago we got a five-year grant from the National Lottery for a piece of work that we had undertaken. This was amazing, and it gave me a moment to think about a five-year plan leading to possible retirement. But can I really retire?!

"Addup continues to grow and develop, although we have stayed relatively small. The CEO and Centre Manager are the only main staff, then we have a team of seasonal staff who manage the projects. We are actually the envy of some other groups I works with for staying small but delivering a lot of services. We don't recruit seasonal staff; they are young people who have grown with Addup – starting as children, training as Volunteer/Mentors and finally becoming regular seasonal staff. So they mostly either have ADHD themselves or are associated with ADHD through a family member.

"We upskill them to know how to conduct themselves in meetings, how to write reports, how to respect management, and above all how to do a great job with the children. This all helps to prepare them for a future in the job market. It works – they learn to manage their ADHD with Addup's support, and they are able to pass on their skills and knowledge to the new children coming through the door. As our first group of young people, now adults with successful lives, come back to visit, many of our current children aspire to follow in their footsteps of going to university, securing apprenticeships, getting respected jobs or becoming an Addup Volunteer/Mentor.

"We are proud of our achievements. We have developed activities that our children need and enjoy, and we have developed our own training packages for schools and other professionals. Our schools training receives positive feedback, mainly for being 'delivered by someone who has lived it not learned it.' We created a parent/child training package for families called 'The Monster Inside', which is often helpful pre-diagnosis. All our training packages are a great success, and are talked about amongst professionals.

"So Addup continues, twenty-five years after we first began to help children and families. Did I think we would survive this long? At times no – but we are determined, we are robust, we don't take no for an answer, we keep knocking on doors until they open and we'll continue to do so for as long as our children need us. I often wonder where my son would be now, or where I would be for that matter, if I hadn't been one of the people who started Addup. Where would many of my children be? How much would it have cost the statutory services if we hadn't intervened? One of our former children, now a successful adult, once said to me: 'I got here because of the support of my family and Addup.' That made me proud of everything we've done.

"Our children are a joy. They are loving, creative and funny with a wicked sense of humour. But you have to listen to them, and you have to think outside the box like they do. They just need a different way of learning. Adapting one thing in a classroom for the ADHD child will actually have a positive impact on every child in that room, so don't see them as different – embrace their ADHD, use it as an asset not a hindrance to learning, and they will surprise you. Give them the same opportunities as every child, give them an incentive to want to please, laugh with them not at them, give them a chance. We can only guide our children. Where they go after that is up to them, but with support and guidance they can all take the right path.

"For all the negativity that surrounds ADHD, there is so much more positivity. I have seen this first-hand, and I have preached about it. My own son is now a Metropolitan Police Officer, and I am proud of him. My other son, who is undiagnosed, lives a successful life in New Zealand. They made it, and so, with the right help and support, can every child with ADHD."

Sheila Keating

CEO of Addup
Mother of Martin
Supervisor of Matt

Part 6: Conclusion

Chapter 31: Summary

This chapter aims to recap the complex challenges facing those affected by attention difficulties. Throughout this book we have addressed a multitude of possible contributing factors, both external and internal, and we have also looked at a wide array of possible strategies, approaches and responses for supporting children and families. There is no 'one size fits all' approach; each child and family brings its own unique personalities, experiences and perceptions of the world into the home and classroom. It is our hope that, by summarising the key points below, we can empower our young people, parents, families and teachers to respond with empathy, a deeper understanding and a toolkit of techniques to try out. Every hurdle that is then cleared successfully is a step closer to the ultimate end goal – a society where ADHD is not only understood, but actively welcomed and celebrated.

> ## Key Point
>
> *There is no 'one size fits all' approach; each child and family brings its own personalities, experiences and perceptions into the home and classroom.*

ADHD is a complex abbreviation

ADHD stands for Attention Deficit Hyperactivity Disorder; however, this initialism can be misleading. As we saw in the early chapters of this book, the condition itself has been recognised in a variety of forms for more than a century, from Sir George Still's description of an "abnormal defect of moral control in children" to the present day where the National Institute of Health and Care Excellence (NICE) recognises the condition and has quashed any lingering doubts as to its existence. The name itself has evolved, and may do so again; however, for now we maintain and work with the description 'ADHD'.

A triad of impairments

It is important to note how the triad of impairments that characterise ADHD – poor attention span, excessive impulsivity and hyperactivity – can be caused by a range of factors; neurological, genetic, environmental and in some cases, developmental injury. These impairments can be seen in varying degrees in all children diagnosed with ADHD, and clinicians currently recognise three sub-types of the disorder:

1. Predominantly hyperactive impulsive type
2. Predominantly inattentive type
3. Combined type (the majority of cases)

Is it just ADHD?

Probably not! As many of 75% of children with ADHD have at least one other diagnosable condition, and almost any condition identified with behaviour or learning can potentially overlap with ADHD. Commonly overlapping (or comorbid) conditions are Autistic Spectrum Disorder (ASD), Conduct Disorder, Oppositional Defiance Disorder (ODD), Tourette's Syndrome, Mood Disorder, Bipolar Disorder, Anxiety Disorder, Sensory Processing Disorder (SPD) and Specific Learning Difficulties (SpLDs) such as dyslexia and dyscalculia.

Boys are more likely to be diagnosed initially with ADHD, with externalising (outward-directed) behaviours driving referrals and crossover conditions being also more externalised. Girls are more likely to have crossover with internalised (inward-directed) conditions, and other diagnoses may be made prior to recognition of ADHD. This hugely complex presentation can make the diagnosis and assessment profile complicated, lengthy and confusing – all the more so as it is a constantly evolving process.

Behaviour is communication – but what is being communicated?

It is important to remember, despite the complexities surrounding the root causes of difficulties that young people with ADHD may experience, that the behaviour being observed is the individual struggling to communicate something to the outside world. It is easy to get bogged down in a search for reasons why; however, we must respond to the situation in front of us and keep at the forefront of our hearts and minds questions like: "What am I being told or shown here? Is my mood having an impact? Are they bored? Do they need to move, or would a break be helpful? Do they understand what I am saying or asking? Can they remember what we did yesterday? Are they hyper-focused on something else? Are they motivated?" Questions like these can help us to change our perceptions and mindset.

Remember, remember

Memory is how our brains understand, organise, store and recall information, and it involves many factors. Before memory can come into play, however, we first need to have been able to pay attention to the information coming our way! Once noticed, the information primarily heads to our short-term memory, then onto our working memory where it is manipulated. Useful processed and organised information is then sent to the long-term memory to be stored.

Contrary to previous beliefs, recent research has shown that people with ADHD actually have stronger short term memory skills than their neurotypical peers, provided their attention difficulties allow information to enter in the first place. It is the working memory that is typically impaired and which requires support. This can be achieved by developing visualisation skills, improving muscle memory, using multisensory approaches, working with patterns and repetition, and aiming for monotasking over multitasking.

Classroom secrets

The key to successfully teaching children with ADHD is preparation. Get to know as much as you can about the child as a learner before they enter your classroom. Draw on the parents, SENCO, previous teachers, extended school staff, pupil passports and pupil voice. This is all critical to being as ready as possible, whilst also maintaining an open mind and not letting a 'label' blur your view of the unique and wonderful individual in front of you. Having a classroom that is organised and purposeful, with adults used wisely and sympathetically to support learners, will also bring you one step closer to a successful teacher-learner relationship.

Positivity and purpose

Whilst maintaining a mindset that all behaviour is communication so as to look for reasons behind visible behaviour, it is also necessary to consider responses to that behaviour – in order to prevent it impacting on wellbeing, relationships, barriers to learning and other people. For behaviour strategies to be successful requires 'buy in' – children must have a strong enough sense of self-esteem and belonging to want to fit with expectations and be part of a community, whether it is a classroom or a family home.

To enable this, adults working with children with ADHD must do all they can to promote a positive relationship, using positive messages around desired behaviours and maintaining consistency and fairness to clarify the purpose of the rules and outcomes being set. Point out children doing the 'right' thing more often than you catch them doing the 'wrong' one, ensure that you work 'with' rather than 'against' them, and steer them away from problematic situations. Always be mindful that children with neurodiverse disorders can be up to three years behind their age-equivalent peers emotionally and socially, and adapt approaches accordingly.

Self-regulate to co-regulate

For a child to have an adult responding to them who has lost control of their emotions and stable state can be a scary thing. It is important to recognise our own mood when supporting a child who is dysregulated, for whatever reason. Regulating our own emotions is necessary before we can support a child in regulating theirs. This may mean that someone else needs to step in and take over to support a child in being able to self-regulate, in order for the adult to be in the best possible emotional state at that moment in time.

> ### Key Point
> *It is important to recognise our own mood; regulating our own emotions is necessary before we can support a child in regulating theirs.*

To successfully self-regulate requires three critical components: sensory processing; executive functioning; and emotional regulation. These are all areas that a child with ADHD can struggle with, and that may also challenge an overwhelmed and stressed adult. Remember – learning together that all feelings are okay is an excellent starting point. "What are our triggers? What do these emotions look and feel like for me, and for you? What strategies can I use to revert to a calm state and how can I prevent myself lapsing into that state again?" These are helpful learning points that can be worked through collaboratively for the benefit of both adult and child.

The 3Rs – relationships are key

When working to develop successful and positive relationships with our young people with ADHD, considering a contemporary version of the '3Rs' – rapport, relationships and resilience – can be a powerful approach. To develop the rapport needed to support a child in bringing themselves back from the brink, the (regulated) adult can consider using eye contact, body positioning (incorporating height/distance and personal space), nodding, facial expression and stillness whilst utilising active listening approaches.

Keeping this rapport can support the relationships that we want to develop between adult and child – our key aim is to prevent a fight or flight response, as bringing a child back from the brink of a storm is far easier, and easier to recover from for all involved, than emerging from the other side of a tornado. Keep an eye on the precursors and respond accordingly utilising mood management strategies to de-escalate. Storms are inevitable, but it is our resilience that helps us to recover and move away from the storm damage.

Collaborative family support

Schools and families must work together to achieve the best outcomes for the young people moving through our education system. At every stage of the journey – from first recognition of the behaviours being communicated, through assessment pathways and key transition points, to developmental milestones and moving on to next education stages, the relationship between school staff and young people and their families should be based on trust, honesty, openness, accessibility, empathy and understanding. Parents are world experts on their children, but school staff are supporting children within a setting that parents are not part of. For this rocky road to be travelled successfully, we must all be headed in the same direction, with the child and family's best interests at heart. Ensuring that every member of the community has a voice, and is heard, will support successful journeys.

Medication

Medication has always been a controversial issue. It should not be seen as the only response to a diagnosis of ADHD, and although medication can be very effective it is only one of the tools available to support children with attention difficulties. ADHD medications fall into two main types – stimulant and non-stimulant. Both work by altering chemical imbalances within the brain, and it can take some time to find the medication that works best in supporting management of an individual child's condition. A process of observation, assessment, trials and balancing benefits against side effects is required before the final situation is evaluated. This requires constant reviews to identify necessary adaptations as children mature and change.

Therapeutic support

In addition to medical support, a range of alternative and additional therapeutic options is available for supporting those impacted by ADHD. Approaches such as counselling, coaching and Cognitive Behavioural Therapy (CBT) can equip young people and families with understanding and strategies to refocus sense of self, anxiety, self-esteem, behaviour patterns, communication, social skills and mood management. Research suggests that CBT is the most effective approach of these three approaches.

The impact of lifestyle choices

While recognising that environmental factors alone cannot cause ADHD, it should be noted that some external factors such as diet, screen time and stress can contribute to more challenging behaviours. Diet is critical to good mental as well as physical health. Working towards maintaining a consistent blood sugar level can only be of benefit; fatty acids in the diet, regular hydration with water, and fish oils can be considered in supporting a healthy mind. In addition to food choices, healthy sleeping is also vital. Many children with ADHD have a sleep disorder, and not getting sufficient sleep can have long term impact on mood, behaviour and health. Working to develop sleep hygiene, while considering intake of caffeine, a fixed sleep schedule, limited screen time and increased exercise within the day, can support healthier sleep schedules as well as helping to maintain a healthy mindset.

Be ready for things to change

Just when you feel you have a handle on things, and are on top of support and management for the person with ADHD in your care, something will change and rock the foundations – both for you and for the child. There will be key transition points where you will need to consider a possible change of approach or strategy, and being prepared is far more comfortable than being blindsided. Be ready for the approach of pivotal events such as the transition between schools, between key stages and between settings. Changes will need to be supported, keeping everyone involved in order to make each transition a success. Be aware that the change from class to class will also require a level of support at the end of each school year. Finally, bear in mind that it is not only the external environment and adults that change; the child is also constantly growing and developing, adding a further layer of transitional complexity.

The reality of living with ADHD

ADHD is a lifelong neurobiological condition that impacts hugely upon many aspects of people's lives and the lives of their families. It is believed that 2-5% of primary aged children have ADHD along with 3-4% of adults (many of them undiagnosed), so awareness needs to extend from schools into the workplace and family homes around the country and the world. That ADHD is more genetically inheritable than breast cancer is a sobering statistic. It is often the case that families living with and supporting children with ADHD through education are also managing and running a home, with the challenges thereby reaching further and deeper into the family unit.

Chapter 32: A last word to parents and carers

Some years ago, at a parent support group meeting on Autism Spectrum Disorder, two parents were overheard talking. One said to the other:

"The doctor says that my son doesn't have autism; he has more ADD."

"ADD – what's that?" said the second parent.

"I'm not exactly sure" replied the first parent. *"I think it stands for Attention Devastation Disorder."*

> ## Key Point
>
> *ADHD is a difference in development, and it is with understanding and responding to this that parents and children often need the most help.*

Though at first glance this may raise a smile, 'devastation' is in many cases an accurate description of the impact that the behaviour of a child with ADHD can have on a family – and that is no laughing matter. For 'devastation', one could equally read 'disruption', 'defiance' or even 'danger'. However, what if the D stood instead for 'difference'? Or, for parents and caregivers, 'desire' or 'determination'?

ADHD is first and foremost a difference in development, and it is with understanding and responding to this that parents and children often need the most help, both at home and at school. Navigating support services is not always easy, but that is where desire and determination can really come to the fore as you seek the best possible support for your child. Focus on the positives, and keep in mind the bigger picture: to produce adults who are capable of initiating the changes we will require as a society tomorrow, we need children and young people who can think and act differently today.

Parenting a child with ADHD can be a hugely rewarding, exciting and fun experience. But it can also be hugely challenging, and for those supporting young people with ADHD on a day-to-day basis, while taking the best possible care of them is of course paramount, it is essential to also pay attention to looking after yourself. It is easy to sacrifice your own wellbeing for theirs, but only by being physically and mentally fit and healthy can you support them to fulfil their potential and live their very best lives.

Be firm in establishing clear ground rules, and give more leeway as the young person's judgment improves. Do not flood a child with small, time-consuming decisions such as what to wear, but where possible seek their opinion on larger matters. Be prepared for the absentmindedness of children with attention problems, and always repeat yourself as if it were the first time. Children with ADHD are not being wilful or stubborn when they forget! Make sure you have the child's attention before making a request, speak slowly, and state it in simple, one-concept commands. Short lists of tasks area excellent ways to help a child remember. Goals should be challenging but always within their capabilities.

Since many children with ADHD are disorganised, they can have difficulty relating events in sequence. Adults may need to quietly ask "who, what, where, and when" questions to get the necessary information. Again, a calm, uncritical manner should be the rule, as it should also be when managing children's difficulties with waiting their turn. Routines are helpful for all children, but they are particularly needed by children with attention problems, so each family should find the schedule for meals, homework, TV and bedtime that suits it best. Help other family members to recognise and understand the young person's differences; this child cannot help being impulsive, loud, forgetful or clumsy, and the patience of siblings with their brother or sister will be of great assistance.

Finally, parents and carers themselves must come to terms with a child's strengths and weaknesses and accept that he or she may need support for many years. Living with the challenges of ADHD can be overwhelming, with a child with ADHD typically hearing 20,000 more negative messages by the end of primary school than their neurotypical peers. Remember to also celebrate, recognise and channel the wealth of positivity that ADHD can bring – a person who is creative and imaginative, quick thinking, enthusiastic, driven and resourceful, empathetic, and emotionally in tune with self and others. Above all, never think of your child as having a 'deficit', 'diagnosis', 'disorder' or 'disability'. He or she is just 'different', and as parents, carers and a wider world we must learn to embrace that.

Chapter 33: A last word to teachers and schools

With the multitude of terms used today to describe various aspects of special educational needs and disability, it is hardly surprising that teachers and schools sometimes feel overwhelmed. Faced with such complexity, what is needed is practical insight into how some children and young people learn differently from their neurotypical peers. This, then, is the focus

Key Point

Fairness in education does not mean treating everybody in exactly the same way; it means giving everybody the same opportunities.

that we have advocated throughout this book: not to dwell on the ADHD label, but instead to consider real-world ways to support those with the developmental differences and traits that characterise the ADHD condition.

Finding the right balance when supporting just two or three very different learners in a class of thirty children can be challenging. However, it can also be an opportunity to adapt tried and tested approaches to children's education, and in some cases to develop new teaching skills. Never forget that while it is easy to spot those overt learners who are more obviously different, there may also be range of more covert learners drifting through their school experience. In some ways ADHD can serve as a useful guide not only for meeting the needs of those students who are directly affected by it, but also for reaching out more effectively to students of all kinds.

A point often raised in training sessions is that if an individual is taught or treated differently in a classroom then the other children are likely to complain that this is unfair. The key issue here is that fairness in education does not mean treating everybody in exactly the same way; it means giving everybody the same opportunities, which means giving each and every individual whatever he or she needs in order to flourish. Another issue to bear in mind is that the classmates of a child with ADHD will already be aware that he or she is somehow different; they just won't know why.

Consider placement – sit the child near the teacher with his or her back to the rest of the class to keep other students out of view. Surround him or her with good role models to provide opportunities for cooperative learning, and place these learners away from distractions like air conditioning units, windows and high traffic areas. Take care with communication – maintain eye contact when giving instructions, avoid multiple requests, make directions clear and concise, and be consistent with daily expectations. Take care when planning and delivering learning – make sure the child understands before beginning a task, and repeat in a calm, positive manner if needed. Make sure the task you are setting is assessing knowledge and skills and not attention span. Give one task at a time, modify assignments and allow extra time as necessary, and monitor progress frequently.

Some say knowledge is power; we prefer to think of it as understanding. Therefore, while we have attempted to help teachers and educators learn more about ADHD and the conditions that commonly co-exist with it, and we have outlined a range of support systems and strategies, this is only the beginning of the process. The real magic happens when, as a teacher or as a whole school, you take every non-ADHD pupil and every non-ADHD parent with you on a journey towards building a culture of acceptance, inclusion and understanding of neurodiversity. Only then can our children and young people with ADHD truly succeed and prosper within our educational systems.

Index of *How to Help* advice

Appendices

Appendix 1: DSM-5 diagnostic criteria[10]

Attention-Deficit/Hyperactivity Disorder (ADHD)

A. A persistent pattern of inattention and/or hyperactivity/impulsivity that interferes with functioning or development, as characterized by (1) and/or (2).

1. **Inattention:** Six (or more) of the following symptoms have persisted for at least 6 months to a degree that is inconsistent with developmental level and that negatively impacts directly on social and academic/occupational activities:

   Note: The symptoms are not solely a manifestation of oppositional behavior, defiance, hostility, or failure to understand tasks or instructions. For older adolescents and adults (age 17 and older), at least five symptoms are required.

   a. Often fails to give close attention to details or makes careless mistakes in schoolwork, at work, or during other activities (e.g., overlooks or misses details, work is inaccurate).

   b. Often has difficulty sustaining attention in tasks or play activities (e.g., has difficulty remaining focused during lectures, conversations, or lengthy reading).

   c. Often does not seem to listen when spoken to directly (e.g., mind seems elsewhere, even in the absence of any obvious distraction).

   d. Often does not follow through on instructions and fails to finish schoolwork, chores, or duties in the workplace (e.g., starts tasks but quickly loses focus and is easily sidetracked).

   e. Often has difficulty organizing tasks and activities (e.g., difficulty managing sequential tasks; difficulty keeping materials and belongings in order; messy, disorganized work; has poor time management; fails to meet deadlines).

   f. Often avoids, dislikes, or is reluctant to engage in tasks that require sustained mental effort (e.g., schoolwork or homework; for older adolescents and adults, preparing reports, completing forms, reviewing lengthy papers).

   g. Often loses things necessary for tasks or activities (e.g., school materials, pencils, books, tools, wallets, keys, paperwork, eyeglasses, mobile telephones).

h. Is often easily distracted by extraneous stimuli (for older adolescents and adults, may include unrelated thoughts).

i. Is often forgetful in daily activities (e.g., doing chores, running errands; for older adolescents and adults, returning calls, paying bills, keeping appointments).

2. **Hyperactivity and impulsivity:** Six (or more) of the following symptoms have persisted for at least 6 months to a degree that is inconsistent with developmental level and that negatively impacts directly on social and academic/occupational activities:

Note: The symptoms are not solely a manifestation of oppositional behavior, defiance, hostility, or failure to understand tasks or instructions. For older adolescents and adults (age 17 and older), at least five symptoms are required.

a. Often fidgets with or taps hands or feet or squirms in seat.

b. Often leaves seat in situations when remaining seated is expected (e.g., leaves his or her place in the classroom, in the office or other workplace, or in other situations that require remaining in place).

c. Often runs about or climbs in situations where it is inappropriate. (Note: In adolescents or adults, may be limited to feeling restless.)

d. Often unable to play or engage in leisure activities quietly.

e. Is often "on the go," acting as if "driven by a motor" (e.g., is unable to be or uncomfortable being still for extended time, as in restaurants, meetings; may be experienced by others as being restless or difficult to keep up with).

f. Often talks excessively.

g. Often blurts out an answer before a question has been completed (e.g., completes people's sentences; cannot wait for turn in conversation).

h. Often has difficulty waiting his or her turn (e.g., while waiting in line).

i. Often interrupts or intrudes on others (e.g., butts into conversations, games, or activities; may start using other people's things without asking or receiving permission; for adolescents and adults, may intrude into or take over what others are doing).

B. Several inattentive or hyperactive-impulsive symptoms were present prior to age 12 years.

C. Several inattentive or hyperactive-impulsive symptoms are present in two or more settings (e.g., at home, school, or work; with friends or relatives; in other activities).

D. There is clear evidence that the symptoms interfere with, or reduce the quality of, social, academic, or occupational functioning.

E. The symptoms do not occur exclusively during the course of schizophrenia or another psychotic disorder and are not better explained by another mental disorder (e.g., mood disorder, anxiety disorder, dissociative disorder, personality disorder, substance intoxication or withdrawal).

Specify whether:

Combined presentation: If both Criterion A1 (inattention) and Criterion A2 (hyperactivity-impulsivity) are met for the past 6 months.

Predominantly inattentive presentation: If Criterion A1 (inattention) is met but Criterion A2 (hyperactivity-impulsivity) is not met for the past 6 months.

Predominantly hyperactive/impulsive presentation: If Criterion A2 (hyperactivity-impulsivity) is met but Criterion A1 (inattention) is not met over the past 6 months.

Specify if:

In partial remission: When full criteria were previously met, fewer than the full criteria have been met for the past 6 months, and the symptoms still result in impairment in social, academic, or occupational functioning.

Specify current severity:

Mild: Few, if any, symptoms in excess of those required to make the diagnosis are present, and symptoms result in only minor functional impairments.

Moderate: Symptoms or functional impairment between "mild" and "severe" are present.

Severe: Many symptoms in excess of those required to make the diagnosis, or several symptoms that are particularly severe, are present, or the symptoms result in marked impairment in social or occupational functioning.

Appendix 2: ADHD support groups

National support groups

ADHD Foundation
The ADHD Foundation is the national ADHD charity for the UK, and the largest user-led ADHD charity in Europe. It promotes a strengths-based approach to living with ADHD and other forms of neurodiversity.

www.adhdfoundation.org.uk

ADDISS
The National Attention Deficit Disorder Information and Support Service provides people-friendly information and resources about ADHD to anyone who needs assistance – parents, sufferers, teachers or health professionals.

www.addiss.co.uk

Addup
Addup was founded to bring families together, to guide parents in the right direction to find the practical help they need for their children, and to promote both public and professional awareness of ADHD.

http://www.addup.co.uk

Living with ADHD
Living with ADHD is designed to support those who come into contact with ADHD – parents, carers and teachers – and to provide resources that help young people to understand and manage their condition.

www.livingwithadhd.co.uk

ADHD Voices
ADHD Voices is a research project that brings the perspectives and experiences of children into international debates around rising child psychiatric diagnoses and the increasing use of drugs in child psychiatry.

www.adhdvoices.com

Patoss
The Professional Association of Teachers of Students with Specific Learning Difficulties is designed for all those concerned with the teaching and support of pupils with learning difficulties such as dyslexia, dyscalculia and ADHD.

www.patoss-dyslexia.org

Adders

Adders aims to promote awareness of ADHD and to provide online information and free practical help to those affected and their families.

www.adders.org

ADD-NI

Originally a support network for children, young people and families, ADD-NI now provides specialist services across Northern Ireland with the aim of promoting and supporting the needs of those affected by ADHD.

www.addni.org

Mindroom

Mindroom is a Scottish special needs charity that supports, informs and empowers children and young people living with learning difficulties.

www.mindroom.org

Local support groups

Below is a selection of regional ADHD support groups. The list is not exhaustive, and many other groups exist on social media and elsewhere.

Brighton

ADHD Aware

www.adhdaware.org.uk

Bristol

Bristol Adult ADHD Support Group

www.aadduk.org

Cambridgeshire

Pinpoint Parent Carer Forum

www.pinpoint-cambs.org.uk

Dundee

Dundee and Angus ADHD Support Group

www.adhddasupport.org

Essex

ADHD+ Support
www.adhd-support.org.uk

Glasgow

ADHD Parent Support West Glasgow
www.adhdglasgow.org

Hertfordshire

ADD-Vance: The ADHD and Autism Trust
www.add-vance.org

Angels Support Group
www.angelssupportgroup.org.uk

Lancashire

ADHD Lancashire
www.adhdlancashire.co.uk

London

Centre for ADHD and Autism Support
www.adhdandautism.org

The London adult ADHD support group
www.sites.google.com/site/joyfivolous/home

Manchester

Manchester Region Attention Deficit Disorder Group
www.maddchester.com

Norfolk

ADHD Norfolk
www.adhdnorfolk.org.uk

West Sussex

The Hyperactive Children's Support Group
www.hacsg.org.uk

References

Aben, B., Stapert, S., & Blokland, A. (2012). About the distinction between working memory and short-term memory. *Frontiers in Psychology*, 3, Article 301.

Achenbach, T. M. (1991). Manual for the Child Behavior Checklist/4-18 and 1991 profile. Burlington, VT: University of Vermont, Department of Psychiatry.

Al-Ghani, K.I. (2008) *The Red Beast: Controlling Anger in Children with Asperger's Syndrome.* London: Jessica Kingsley.

Alloway, T., (2016). What is the link between ADHD and working memory? *Psychology Today*, 27 June 2016

Amen, D.G. (2020). 9 Foods to Supercharge Your Brain Health. ADDitude. Accessed at https://www.additudemag.com/slideshows/adhd-nutrition-brain/

American Psychiatric Association. (2013). *Diagnostic and Statistical Manual of Mental Disorders (5th ed.).* Arlington, VA: APA.

Baker, L. & Cantwell, D.P. (1992). Attention deficit disorder and speech/language disorders. *Comprehensive Mental Health Care*, 2(1), 3-16.

Barkley, R. A. (1981). *Hyperactive children: A handbook for diagnosis and treatment.* New York: Guilford Press.

Barkley, R. A. (1997) *ADHD and The Nature of Self-Control.* New York: Guilford Press.

Barkley, R.A. (1997). Attention-deficit/hyperactivity disorder, self-regulation, and time: toward a more comprehensive theory. *Journal of Developmental and Behavioral Pediatrics* 18:271–279.

Barkley, R. A. (2006). *Attention-deficit hyperactivity disorder: A handbook for diagnosis and treatment* (3rd ed.). New York: Guilford Press.

Boot, N., Nevicka, B., & Baas, M. (2017) Subclinical symptoms of attention-deficit/hyperactivity disorder (ADHD) are associated with specific creative processes. *Personality and Individual Differences, 114/1: 73-81*

Burron, K., & Curtis, M. (2012). *The Incredible 5-Point Scale: Assisting Students in Understanding Social Interactions and Controlling Their Emotional Responses.* Shawnee KS.: AAPC Publishing.

Canady, V. (2020). FDA approves first video game Rx treatment for children with ADHD. Mental Health Weekly. Accessed at https://doi.org/10.1002/mhw.32423.

Chang Y., Liu S., Yu H. & Lee Y. (2012). Effect of acute exercise on executive function in children with attention deficit hyperactivity disorder. *Archives of Clinical Neuropsychology* 27 225–237.

Connors, C. K. (1997). *Conners' Rating Scales-Revised Technical Manual.* North Tonawanda, NY.

Cowan N. (2001). The magical number four in short-term memory: a reconsideration of mental storage capacity. *Behavioral and Brain Sciences* 24, 87–114.

Crichton, A. (1798) An inquiry into the nature and origin of mental derangement: comprehending a concise system of the physiology and pathology of the human mind and a history of the passions and their effects.

Dale, E. (1946). *Audio-Visual Methods in Teaching.* New York: Dryden Press.

Department for Education and Department of Health and Social Care (2014) Special educational needs and disability code of practice: 0 to 25 years. Available at: https://www.gov.uk/government/publications/send-code-of-practice-0-to-25

Dodson, W. (2021) *ADHD and Sleep Problems: This is Why You're Always So Tired.* ADDitude

Dodson, W. (2021) *ADHD and the Epidemic of Shame.* Attitude magazine. Url: https://www.additudemag.com/slideshows/adhd-and-shame/

Dolcourt J.L. (2000). Commitment to change: a strategy for promoting educational effectiveness. *Journal of Continuing Education in the Health Professions.* 20: 156-63.

Dweck, C.S. (2006). *Mindset: The new psychology of success.* New York: Random House.

Dyall, S.C. (2015). Long-chain omega-3 fatty acids and the brain: a review of the independent and shared effects of EPA, DPA and DHA. *Frontiers in Aging Neuroscience*, 7: 52.

Gershon, J. (2002) A meta-analytic review of gender differences in ADHD. *Journal of Attention Disorders* 5(3):143-154.

Glasser, W. (1999). *Choice Theory*. New York: HarperPerennial.

Gray, C. (1994). *Comic Strip Conversations: Illustrated Interactions that Teach Conversation Skills to Students with Autism and Related Disorders*. Jenison, MI.: Jenison Public Schools.

Hebb, D.O. (1949). *The Organization of Behavior*. New York: John Wiley & Sons.

Hemmi M.H., Wolke, D., & Schneider, S. (2011). Associations between problems with crying, sleeping and/or feeding in infancy and long-term behavioural outcomes in childhood: a meta-analysis. *Archives of Disease in Childhood* 96: 622-9.

Hjalmarsdottir, F. (2020). Does nutrition play a role in ADHD? Healthline. Accessed at https://www.healthline.com/nutrition/nutrition-and-adhd

Hoffmann, H. (1846) Der Struwwelpeter. Oder lustige Geschichten und drollige Bilder für Kinder von 3 bis 6 Jahren. Loewes, Stuttgart: Frankfurter Originalausgabe.

Hospital Pharmacy Europe. (2020) *Diagnosis and Management of ADHD: Summary of NICE guidance*. Published 18th August 2020.

Ivry, R.B., & Fiez, J.A. (2000). Cerebellar contributions to cognition and imagery. In M.S. Gazzaniga (Ed.), *The new cognitive neurosciences* (2nd ed). Cambridge, MA: MIT Press.

Kelsi Inclusion Support Service Kent. https://www.kelsi.org.uk/special-education-needs/special-educational-needs/the-mainstream-core-standards

Kennedy Krieger Institute. (2021). Is it ADHD or Typical Toddler Behavior? Ten Early Signs of ADHD Risk in Preschool Age Children. Retrieved from https://www.kennedykrieger.org/stories/Is-it-adhd-or-typical-toddler-behavior-ten-early-signs-adhd-risk-preschool-age-children

Kohlberg, J. & Nadeau, K. (2002) *ADD-Friendly Ways to Organize Your Life*. New York: Brunner-Routledge.

Kramer F. & Pollnow, H. (1932) Über eine hyperkinetische Erkrankung im Kindesalter. Aus der Psychiatrischen und Nerven-Klinik der Charité in Berlin. Mschr Psychiat Neurol. 82:21–40.

Kuypers, L. (2011). *The Zones of Regulation: A Curriculum Designed to Foster Self-Regulation and Emotional Control*. Santa Clara, CA.: Think Social Publishing.

Lamb, B. (2009). Lamb Inquiry Special Educational Needs and Parental Confidence. Annesley: DCSF Publications.

Lands, B. (2017). Highly unsaturated fatty acids (HUFA) mediate and monitor food's impact on health. *Prostaglandins and Other Lipid Mediators, 133*: 4-10.

Loewen, R., & Pliner, P. (1999). Effects of prior exposure to palatable and unpalatable novel foods on children's willingness to taste other novel foods. *Appetite, 32*.

Mahon A.D. et al. (2013). Acute exercise effects on measures of attention and impulsivity in children with ADHD. *Journal of Educational and Developmental Psychology*. 3(2):65.

McCarney, S.B. & House, S.N. (2019). *Attention Deficit Disorder Evaluation Scale* (ADDES-5). Columbia, MO, Hawthorne Educational Services.

McKnight, J. (1989). Parents are 'Experts' on Their Children. EducationWeek opinion piece, November 29th 1989.

Mehrabian, A. (1981). *Silent messages: Implicit communication of emotions and attitudes (2d ed.)*. Belmont, CA.: Wadsworth Publishing.

Miller, G. (1956). The magical number seven, plus or minus two: Some limits on our capacity for processing information. *The psychological review*, 63, 81-97.

Pachecho, D. (2021) *ADHD and Sleep*. Sleep Foundation.

Paruthi S. et al. (2016). Recommended amount of sleep for pediatric populations: a consensus statement of the AASM. Journal of Clinical Sleep Medicine 12(6): 785–786.

Power, T. J., & Ikeda, M. J. (1996). The clinical utility of behavior rating scales: Comments on the diagnostic assessment of ADHD. *Journal of School Psychology*, 34(4), 379-385.

Safren, S. et al. (2010). Cognitive behavioral therapy vs relaxation with educational support for medication-treated adults with ADHD and persistent symptoms: a randomized controlled trial. *Journal of the American Medical Association* 304 (8), 875-880.

Schlueb, M. (2017) *ADHD Kids Can Be Still – If They're Not Straining Their Brains.* UCF Today.

Sherman, C., Ramsay, J.R., & Barrow, K. (2021). *How CBT Dismantles ADHD Negativity: Cognitive Behavioral Therapy Overview.* ADDitude. Accessed at https://www.additudemag.com/cognitive-behavioral-therapy-for-adhd/

Slavin, R.E. (1994). *Educational Psychology: Theory into Practice.* 4th ed. Boston: Allyn and Bacon.

Still, G.F. (1902). Some abnormal psychical conditions in children: the Goulstonian lectures. Lancet. 1: 1008-1012.

University of Illinois at Urbana-Champaign. *A Walk In The Park Improves Attention In Children With ADHD.* ScienceDaily. 15 October 2008.

Wajszilber D. et al. (2018). Sleep disorders in patients with ADHD; Impact and Management challenges. *Nature and Science of Sleep* 10: 453-480.